D0842021

PEACE

UNDERSTANDING BIBLICAL THEMES

COVENANT
Steven L. McKenzie

INCARNATION
Jon L. Berquist

PEACE
Walter Brueggemann

SABBATH AND JUBILEE
Richard H. Lowery

PEACE

WALTER BRUEGGEMANN

Chalice Press®
St. Louis, Missouri

© Copyright 2001 by Walter Brueggemann

All rights reserved. No part of this book may be reproduced without written permission from Chalice Press, P.O. Box 179, St. Louis, MO 63166-0179.

Bible quotations, unless otherwise noted, are from the *New Revised Standard Version Bible,* copyright 1989, Division of Christian Education of the National Council of the Churches of Christ in the United States of America. Used by permission. All rights reserved.

Those quotations marked RSV are from the *Revised Standard Version of the Bible,* copyright 1952 [2nd edition, 1971], by the Division of Christian Education of the National Council of the Churches of Christ in the United States of America. Used by permission. All rights reserved.

Cover and interior design: Elizabeth Wright

This book is printed on acid-free, recycled paper.

Visit Chalice Press on the World Wide Web at
www.chalicepress.com

10 9 8 7 6 5 4 3 2 1   01 02 03 04 05 06

Library of Congress Cataloging–in–Publication Data

Brueggemann, Walter.
    Peace / Walter Brueggemann.
        p.   cm. — (Understanding biblical themes)
    Rev. ed. of : Living toward a vision.
    ISBN 0-8272-3828-2
    1. Peace—Biblical teaching. 2. Church and the world. I. Brueggemann, Walter. Living toward a vision. II. Title. III. Series.
BS680.P4 B78 2001
261.8'73 — dc21   2001000773
                                                                CIP

Printed in the United States of America

CONTENTS

PART FIVE: *SHALOM* PERSONS

PREFACE

I am pleased that Jon L. Berquist at Chalice Press has agreed to republish this book, which has been out of print at the United Church Press for a spell. Although the papers in this book are to some extent dated, I hope and believe that they continue to have resonance for those in the church who care about public dimensions of the gospel and the ministry of the church. The papers given here are for the most part ad hoc presentations, offered orally in response to invitations in various church programs. Without being very intentional about it, it is clear in retrospect that my involvement in such ad hoc presentations, with an eye on missional "relevance," set me on a course of interpretation that has characteristically bent me toward church practice; consequently, I have cared about but held loosely the more critical side of scholarship, in which one must of necessity engage if one is to be a responsible, informed interpreter. These essays indicate a sort of choice I have consistently exercised about the interface of the critical and the contemporary ecclesial facets of interpretation.

I

These essays, aimed at church practice, arose in a difficult time in U.S. society, the main contours of which are well known. The defining events in the United States in the late 1960s and early 1970s included

1

the civil rights movement, featuring both Martin Luther King, Jr., and Malcolm X; the Vietnam War, which King had the temerity to link to civil rights, the Kennedy and King assassinations; and the Watergate scandal, which placed in jeopardy old patterns of institutional life. This cluster of events created a sense of openness to newness, a suspicion of old patterns of power, a resistance to old patterns of authority, and a fresh sense of the possible.

The theological manifestation of this peculiar time and theological response to it was one of hope that was more than a little tinged with romanticism. Perhaps the most typical or shaping influence was the book by Harvey Cox *The Secular City,* which was widely read in that context. Cox offered a celebrative reception of the secular that was something like "the dawning of the Age of Aquarius." Cox's sociotheology was echoed in popular form by Sister Coretta, who in the wake of Vatican II, made an industry out of producing banners with quasireligious affirmations about the new possibilities before us as old things were breaking open.

My church rootage is in the United Church of Christ, which in the 1960s was, at the national level, still in the mood of its initial euphoria, having been formed in 1957. That founding enthusiasm, moreover, was fed by the more general theological mood of the period. In its educational offerings, the national offices of the UCC had resolved to be intentionally avant-garde both in the visible appearance of its curriculum materials and in the theological assumptions and articulations that received a venturesomely fresh voicing. Among other things, the educational enterprise latched onto *shalom* as a symbol and mantra of a new wave of theological opinion and nurture. Although there was biblical and theological study behind the accent on *shalom,* it is fair to say that it became a popular slogan that came to signal all things new.

Specifically, appeal to *shalom* represented a commitment to the well-being of the world that was not to linger over churchy, parochial things; after the manner of Cox's *secular,* the term *shalom* attested to God's goodwill and transformative engagement for the sake of the world. The accent in the UCC, moreover, did not reflect long on God's enactment of *shalom;* in characteristic UCC fashion, interpretation turned a theological accent into an ethical emphasis on *human* enactment of well-being in the world. Commitment to *shalom,* to which many of us gravitated passionately, was on the romantic side and lacked a critical edge, a liberal propensity to think that if we all said well and we all did well, all would be well. The short shelf life of such romanticism is signaled by the fact that Cox himself soon moved sharply away from the secular and has since that time been pondering the depth, power, and rootage of particular theological and church traditions.

Thus, an embracive *shalom* from that odd moment in our social history is to be assessed, I judge, as a great gain in a move beyond traditionalism. It was, however, a gain that was not critical of itself (and its romanticism) as it was so readily critical of tradition and traditionalism. An accent on *shalom,* as it turned out, eventuated in a kind of well-meaning theological liberalism that from a perspective of "post-liberal" theology seems thin indeed. But then, one cannot second-guess the theological work that is done in good faith and seriousness in another context, even if that other context is not far removed in time.

II

Given that troubled time, given a more or less euphoric theological response to the troubled time, and given my own deep engagement at the time with the *shalom* accent of my church, I pondered then and have pondered much since then how different the course of our church life (and these essays) might have been had the large notion of *shalom* been more directly related to *mishpat,* that is, *justice.* It is of course a truism to say "no peace without justice," or "no peace without justice first." And perhaps that was all implied at the time in the term *shalom,* with *mishpat* as a subset of *shalom.* It was not, however, in any critical way recognized as a real and indispensable component of *shalom.* To ponder *shalom-cum-mishpat,* peace with and through justice, has led me to the following awarenesses:

1. In our account of *shalom,* a Jewish notion was happily appropriated that defied all the dualisms (especially worldly/religious) common in conventional thinking. But the Jewish reality of *shalom* as a work in progress always marked by fraction and incompleteness was lacking. If that Jewish realism and capacity for disjunction had been realized, our church use of the term might have been less romantic.

2. Taken by itself and without appropriate Jewish grounding, the notion of *shalom* lends itself to a passion for equilibrium, a sense of

system in which all the parts cohere. Such an innocent usage reflects a liberal propensity to settle for an organic view of social wholeness reflective of the social theories of Émile Durkheim and Talcott Parsons. On offer was a kind of wholeness that was unaware of the fact that every such "new world order," in whatever scope, is always an order of privilege and commensurate exclusivism. A hope for a future well-being that quickly becomes a sort of "realized eschatology" tends not to reckon with the reality of evil as it shows up in exclusionary and exploitative social practice.

3. Given the unwitting commitment to a sociology of equilibrium, it would be fair to say that the bite of Marxian analysis was absent in the romantic euphoria of the moment. Of course, Marxian analysis could not be avoided by anyone who thought well and faithfully about the future. For the most part, however, these interpretive categories came late to church interpretation. Of course there arose about the same time the remarkable developments in Roman Catholic Latin American theology that centered in the work of Gustavo Gutiérrez.[1] That brave band of church theologians produced the astonishing formulations of Medellin and Puebla on "God's preferential option for the poor." And while liberal Protestant sympathies had long run in that direction, for the most part there was missing among us the focus and incisiveness of such a critical formulation. For myself, the turning point came with José Miranda's *Marx and the Bible*[2] whose Marxian analysis was fleshed out in critical form by the magisterial work of Norman Gottwald, in *The Tribes of Yahweh*.[3] What had been intuitive and implicit in a liberal perspective was now made explicit and concrete; but for the most part that critical awareness did not yet connect to the liberal narrative of *shalom* in the mid-1970s that was still more wish and hope than hard, disciplined, critical resolve.

4. The "new world order" of *shalom* in the Christian Old Testament is largely a function of royal ideology. It deals in sweeping summaries from above. That is, it tends to be an ordering fostered by and beneficial to those in charge, characteristically the urban elite who managed the

[1]Gustavo Gutiérrez, *A Theology of Liberation: History, Politics, and Salvation* (Maryknoll, N.Y.: Orbis Books, 1973).

[2]José Miranda, *Marx and the Bible: The Critique of the Philosophy of Oppression* (Maryknoll, N.Y: Orbis Books, 1974).

[3]Norman K. Gottwald, *The Tribes of Yahweh: A Sociology of the Religion of Liberated Israel 1250-1050 B.C.* (Maryknoll, N.Y.: Orbis Books, 1979; 2d ed., Sheffield: Sheffield Academic Press, 1999).

advantages of wealth and technology.[4] Such a systemic perspective tends to run roughshod over the "details" of those who are not "with the program" and who therefore drop out of all statistical reassurances.

It is for that reason that *shalom* is not much on the lips of the criticizing prophets of ancient Israel, except in an occasional anticipatory utterance. Where the prophets engage in present tense social analysis, they do not use the term, for the term bespeaks a systems approach that defaults on "the less fortunate," who are made less fortunate precisely by the romanticizing large-scale order of well-being. The prophets characteristically use the language of "justice and righteousness" that seldom celebrates present equilibrium, but that regularly advocates a disruption of the present equilibrium in more or less revolutionary fashion to redress the injustice that *shalom* covers over.

5. *Shalom* at its most critical can function as a theology of hope, a large-scale promissory vision of what will one day surely be. As a vision of an assured future, the substance of *shalom* is crucial, for it can be a resource against both despair and an overly eager settlement for an unfinished system. But when that vision of the future becomes "present tense," and any present order is equated with that future, *shalom* inevitably results in a self-congratulatory distortion of the present. The most obvious case in point is Francis Fukuyama's book *The End of History*, which equates present democratic capitalism with the largest human hopes.[5] But what Fukuyama crassly asserts on a global scale was also seductive in more modest church rhetoric that failed to maintain a clear distinction between present gifts and expected, promised well-being. Present gifts are always fractured and incomplete when confused with expectations.

III

The occasion for writing this new introduction has been an opportunity for me to return to the texts on *shalom,* of which I will mention three that seem to me suggestive and important in light of the foregoing:

---

[4]I refer, in the first instance, to "urban elites" in that ancient world of "Canaanite city-states." But of course the catagory pertains in our contemporary reading and analyses as well.
[5]Francis Fukuyama, *The End of History and the Last Man* (New York: The Free Press, 1992).

1. Psalm 85 ends with an immense promise:

> Surely his salvation is at hand
>   for those who fear him,
>   that his glory may dwell in our land.
> *Steadfast love* and *faithfulness* will meet;
>   *righteousness* and *peace* will kiss each other.
> *Faithfulness* will spring up from the ground,
>   and *righteousness* will look down from the sky.
> The LORD will give what is good,
>   and our land will yield its increase.
> *Righteousness* will go before him,
>   and will make a path for his steps (vv. 9–13)

This vision of well-being gathers together Israel's remarkable vocabulary of fidelity (steadfast love, faithfulness, righteousness, peace), all of which will be enacted as God's "salvation."[6] That is, the future will be a gift of God's transformative, disruptive assertion. The future is indeed marked by *shalom,* but the *shalom* of verse 10 is situated in the covenantal terms of *steadfast love, faithfulness,* and *righteousness.* Insofar as *shalom* is a new order, it is a new order marked by the neighborly engagement of ground and sky, heaven and earth, God and people.

Behind the assurance, however, is the petition of verses 4–7:

> Restore us again, O God of our salvation,
>   and put away your indignation toward us.
> Will you be angry with us forever?
> Will you prolong your anger to all generations?
> Will you not revive us again,
>   so that your people may rejoice in you?
> Show us your steadfast love, O LORD,
>   and grant us your salvation.

That is, the oracle of vision is evoked by a prayer of petition out of present crisis. The prayer is voiced by people in dire straits; the rhetoric of "restore us again" in verse 4 may suggest exile. That setting is important because it means that there can be no confusion of present and future. *Shalom* marked by fidelity is promised, but it clearly is not in hand.

---

[6]Cf. Walter Brueggemann, *Theology of the Old Testament: Testimony, Dispute, Advocacy* (Minneapolis: Fortress Press, 1997), 223–24. See also Brueggemann, *Deep Memory, Exuberant Hope: Contested Truth in a Post-Christian World,* ed. Patrick D. Miller (Minneapolis: Fortress Press, 2000), 108–9.

2. The same promise to exiles is voiced in the prose assurance of Jeremiah 29:11–14:

> For surely I know the plans I have for you, says the LORD, plans for your *welfare* and not for harm, to give you a future with hope. Then when you call upon me and come and pray to me, I will hear you. When you search for me, you will find me; if you seek me with all your heart, I will let you find me, says the LORD, and I will restore your fortunes and gather you from all the nations and all the places where I have driven you, says the LORD, and I will bring you back to the place from which I sent you into exile.

This passage as well is a divine promise to Israel in exile. Israel's present tense is one of displacement and defeat. The oracle invites Israel to look past its present into a future grounded only in God's reliability. The specific content of that future is to come "back to the place," that is, a homecoming. The phrasing of "restore your fortunes" is parallel to Psalm 85:1. The concern here is that YHWH has a plan for your *shalom,* tellingly rendered in the NRSV as "welfare." The future is an assured well-being for the entire community that is a total contrast to the present, assured only by the trustworthiness of the one who promises.

3. Micah 5:2–5a, a text that occurs regularly in the church lectionary for Advent, anticipates *shalom* in a contested arena of power:

> But you, O Bethlehem of Ephrathah,
>   who are one of the little clans of Judah,
> from you shall come forth for me
>   one who is to rule in Israel,
> whose origin is from of old,
>   from ancient days.
> Therefore he shall give them up until the time
>   when she who is in labor has brought forth;
> then the rest of his kindred shall return
>   to the people of Israel.
> And he shall stand and feed his
>   flock in the strength of the LORD,
>   in the majesty of the name of the LORD his God.
> And they shall live secure, for now he shall be great

to the ends of the earth;
and he shall be the one of *peace.*

This text anticipates a peasant leader from Bethlehem who will rule and bring *shalom* to the realm. That leader, moreover, will confound even the Assyrian Empire. This passage, in subsequent reading, is clearly taken as "messianic." In Israel's own reading, the poem refers to a Davidic king. In Christian reading, it is an anticipation of Jesus. For our purposes it is enough to see that *shalom* is the work of a God-authorized human agent who will enact social welfare, security, and well-being in a way that is quite concrete and material.

All three texts attest to a new future that will displace a negative present tense. The contrast between now and then is also a contrast between a *context of despair* under imperial domination and a *coming context of assured well-being* in an environment of freedom. Attentiveness to this contrast of now and then is enough to protect against a "realized eschatology" that romantically collapses promised future into occupied present. The third text in particular bespeaks social criticism and analysis, for the peasant locus of *shalom* to be enacted contrasts sharply with the practice of urban elites who foster an ideology of undifferentiated present-tense *shalom.*

IV

We are a good bit less romantic about promised well-being than we were in the uncritical euphoria at the time these essays were prepared. Now, however, in an ocean of consumer goods, we run the risk of being narcotized so that we do not notice the socioeconomic disparities that give the lie to "new world order." My own church tradition at the national level is now immensely preoccupied with the sorry U.S. history of racism and offers as an antidote "multiculturalism." It is possible to discern, however, that the current emphasis is almost exclusively on *political* redress of racism. At the same time, the church seems incapable of or unwilling to raise *economic* issues, perhaps because our church leadership (of which I am a part) is so economically advantaged as to make economic issues preferably unnoticed. The problem of singular focus on the *political* without the *economic* is that issues devolve to sheer matters of power, without a commensurate effort about shared destiny that requires a recovered communalism of cruelty and generosity concerned with fidelity as much as power.

However, if William Julius Wilson is in any way correct in his insistence that the major issues now concern *class* even more than *race*, a focus on political *shalom* without economic *mishpat* tends to conceal class issues.[7] And so I now wonder if perhaps my church tradition is at present replicating the uncritical practice of the 1970s, only this time the new world order *(shalom)* is "multicultural." The question permits no single answer, but suggests that we will continue to be haunted, as are these essays, by the fact that the text characteristically shatters our preferred modes of management. The text runs beyond our frail powers of imagination and our lame courage before the "costs of discipleship" (to use Bonhoeffer's familiar phrase). *Shalom* is still promised by God. Our capacity to await it, however, requires a greater attentiveness to our broken present than we are mostly wont to give; it is a brokenness that takes many forms and leaves all broken, not just some.

For all of that, I am glad for my membership in the United Church of Christ and for its continuing struggle for faithfulness. That struggle currently takes shape differently from that of the time of these essays. But, of course, the issues persist in all their intense demand. In my original preface to the book I named and thanked a number of people who nurtured me and the book. I still thank them along with many more recent comrades in the church. Among those, of course, Charles McCollough stands first for his long-term commitment to the book. Our technological society is currently against "the vision thing," which is why our text work is so urgent, our embrace of it so subversive, and our readiness so hesitant.

Walter Brueggemann
Columbia Theological Seminary
Third Week in Lent, 2000

---

[7]William Julius Wilson, *The Declining Significance of Race: Blacks and Changing American Institutions* (Chicago: University of Chicago Press, 1980).

PART ONE

A Vision of *Shalom*

1

LIVING TOWARD A VISION

I will give you your rains in their season, and the land shall yield its produce, and the trees of the field shall yield their fruit. Your threshing shall overtake the vintage, and the vintage shall overtake the sowing; you shall eat your bread to the full, and live securely in your land. And I will grant peace in the land, and you shall lie down, and no one shall make you afraid; I will remove dangerous animals from the land, and no sword shall go through your land.

LEVITICUS 26:4–6

For he is our peace; in his flesh he has made both groups into one and has broken down the dividing wall, that is, the hostility between us.

EPHESIANS 2:14

The central vision of world history in the Bible is that all of creation is one, every creature in community with every other, living in harmony and security toward the joy and well-being of every other creature. *In the community of faith in Israel,* this vision is expressed in the affirmation that Abraham is father of all Israel and every person is his child (see Genesis 15:5; Isaiah 41:8; 51:2). Israel has a vision of all people drawn into community around the will of its God (Isaiah 2:2–4).[1] *In the New Testament, the church* has a parallel vision of all persons being drawn under the lordship and fellowship of Jesus (Matthew 28:16–20; John 12:32) and therefore into a single community (Acts 2:1–11). As if those visions were not sweeping enough, the most staggering expression of the vision is that *all persons* are *children of a single family,* members of a single tribe, heirs of a single hope, and bearers of a single destiny, namely, the care and management of all God's creation.

That persistent vision of joy, well-being, harmony, and prosperity is not captured in any single word or idea in the Bible; a cluster of words is required to express its many dimensions and subtle nuances: love, loyalty, truth, grace, salvation, justice, blessing, righteousness. But the term that in recent discussions has been used to summarize that controlling vision is *shalom.* Both in such discussion[2] and in the Bible itself, it bears tremendous freight—the freight of a dream of God that resists all our tendencies to division, hostility, fear, drivenness, and misery.

Shalom is the substance of the biblical vision of one community embracing all creation. It refers to all those resources and factors that make communal harmony joyous and effective. Ezekiel in a visionary passage expresses its meaning:

> I will make with them a covenant of *shalom* and banish wild beasts from the land, so that they may dwell securely in the wilderness and sleep in the woods. And I will make them and the places round about my hill a blessing; and I will send down the showers in their season; they shall be showers of blessing. And the trees of the field shall yield their fruit, and the earth shall yield its increase, and they shall be secure in their land. They shall no more be a prey to the nations, nor shall the beasts of the land devour them; they shall dwell securely, and none shall make them afraid. And I will provide for them plantations of *shalom.* (Ezekiel 34:25–29a, author's translation)

---

[1] Cf. Walter Brueggemann, *Theology of the Old Testament: Testimony, Dispute, Advocacy* (Minneapolis: Fortress Press, 1997), 501.

[2] See J. C. Hoekendijk, *The Church Inside Out,* trans. Isaac C. Rottenberg, Adventures in Faith (Philadelphia: Westminster Press, 1966); and Johannes Pedersen, *Israel: Its Life and Culture,* I-II (Oxford: Oxford University Press, 1926), 263–65.

The origin and the destiny of God's people are to be on the road of *shalom,* which is to live out of joyous memories and toward greater anticipations.

This passage from Ezekiel and the one from Leviticus quoted at the beginning of the chapter show *shalom* in all its power. It is well-being that exists in the very midst of threats—from sword and drought and wild animals. It is well-being of a material, physical, historical kind, not idyllic "pie in the sky," but "salvation" in the midst of trees and crops and enemies—in the very places where people always have to cope with anxiety, to struggle for survival, and to deal with temptation. It is well-being of a very personal kind—the address in Leviticus 26 is to a single person, but it is also deliberately corporate. If there is to be well-being, it will not be just for isolated, insulated individuals; it is, rather, security and prosperity granted to a whole community—young and old, rich and poor, powerful and dependent. Always we are all in it together. Together we stand before God's blessings and together we receive the gift of life, if we receive it at all. *Shalom* comes only to the inclusive, embracing community that excludes none.

The vision of wholeness, which is the supreme will of the biblical God, is the outgrowth of a covenant of *shalom* (see Ezekiel 34:25), in which persons are bound not only to God but to one another in a caring, sharing, rejoicing community with none to make them afraid.

Dimensions of *Shalom*

The scope of this communal vision is an important element in understanding its power. In its most inclusive dimension it is *a vision encompassing all reality,* expressed in the mystery and majesty of creation images:

[without *shalom*]

The earth was a formless void and darkness covered the face of the deep. (Genesis 1:2a)

[with *shalom*]

The wolf shall live with the lamb,
    the leopard shall lie down with the kid,
the calf and the lion and the fatling together,
    and a little child shall lead them.

> The cow and the bear shall graze,
>   their young shall lie down together;
>   and the lion shall eat straw like the ox...
> They will not hurt or destroy
>   on all my holy mountain. (Isaiah 11:6–7, 9a)

[from chaos to *shalom*]

> A great windstorm arose, and the waves beat into the boat, so that the boat was already being swamped...and they woke him up and said to him, "Teacher, do you not care that we are perishing?" He woke up and rebuked the wind, and said to the sea, "Peace! Be still!" Then the wind ceased, and there was a dead calm. (Mark 4:37–39)

The Greek word translated *peace* here means *quiet* rather than *shalom*, but the passage still applies. The storm at sea represents all the same ominous, chaotic forces presented in Genesis 1:2. And the word of Jesus in Mark serves the same purpose as the hovering spirit of God in Genesis 1:2, namely, to bring fundamental disorder under God's rule—into harmony—so that light, life, and joy become possible. Creation in Genesis and by Jesus (see Colossians 1:17) is the establishment of *shalom* in a universe that apart from God's rule is disordered, unproductive, and unfulfilling.

In the same symbolic word, the messianic vision of Isaiah (11:6–9) is of a world in which creation is reconciled and harmony appears between children and snakes, among all kinds of natural enemies.[3] *Shalom* is creation time, when all God's creation eases up on hostility and destruction and finds another way of relating. No wonder creation culminates in the peace and joy of the Sabbath (Genesis 2:1–4a) when all lie down and none make them afraid. No wonder our most familiar Sabbath blessing ends: "The LORD lift up his countenance upon you. and give you peace *(shalom)*" (Numbers 6:26), for the benediction is the affirmation of Sabbath, the conclusion of creation, when harmony has been brought to all the warring elements in our existence.

A second dimension of *shalom* is the *historic political community.* Absence of *shalom* and lack of harmony are expressed in social disorder as evidenced in economic inequality, judicial perversion, and political oppression and exclusivism. Of course, the prophets speak boldly against such disruption of community, which is the absence of *shalom*:

---

[3]Cf. Brueggemann, *Theology of the Old Testament*, 528–51.

Alas for those who devise wickedness
    and evil deeds on their beds!...
They covet fields, and seize them;
    houses, and take them away;
they oppress householder and house. (Micah 2:1–2)

Hear this word, you cows of Bashan,
    who are on Mount Samaria,
who oppress the poor, who crush the needy,
    who say to their husbands,
        "Bring something to drink!" (Amos 4:1)

These offenses are viewed by the prophets not simply as ethical violations but as the disruption of God's intention for *shalom,* the perversion of the community God wills for people in history. Their call is continually a call for righteousness and justice:

Seek good and not evil, that you may live;
...Hate evil and love good,
    and establish justice in the gate.(Amos 5:14–15a)

Wash yourselves; make yourselves clean;
    remove the evil of your doings
    from before my eyes;
cease to do evil,
    learn to do good;
seek justice,
    rescue the oppressed,
defend the orphan,
    plead for the widow. (Isaiah 1:16–17)

The doing of righteousness and justice results in the building of viable community, that is, *shalom,* in which the oppressed and disenfranchised have dignity and power.

Depart from evil, and do good;
    seek peace *(shalom),* and pursue it. (Psalm 34:14)

Then justice will dwell in the wilderness,
    and righteousness abide in the fruitful field.
The effect of righteousness will be peace *(shalom),*
    and the result of righteousness, quietness and trust forever.
        (Isaiah 32:16–17)

The consequence of justice and righteousness is *shalom,* an enduring Sabbath of joy and well-being. But the alternative is injustice and oppression, which lead inevitably to turmoil and anxiety, with no chance of well-being (Isaiah 48:22; 57:21).

Jesus' ministry to the excluded (see Luke 4:16–21) was the same, the establishment of community between those who were excluded and those who had excluded them. His acts of healing the sick, forgiving the guilty, raising the dead, and feeding the hungry are all actions of reestablishing God's will for *shalom* in a world gone chaotic by callous self-seeking.

The cosmic and historical-political aspects of *shalom* point to a third dimension, which the Bible usually assumes but does not discuss. It is the *shalom* sense of well-being experienced by *the person* who lives a caring, sharing, joyous life in community. By way of contrast, covetousness is presented as one aspect of the self-seeking life that is never satiated but always pursues selfish security only to discover that it leads to destruction:

> "Because of the iniquity of his covetousness
> I was angry, I smote him,
> I hid my face and was angry…
> *Shalom, shalom,* to the far and to the near, says the
>   Lord;
> and I will heal him.
> But the wicked are like the tossing sea;
> for it cannot rest,
> and its waters toss up mire and dirt.
> There is no *shalom,* says my God, for the wicked."
>   (Isaiah 57:17, 19–21, author's translation; compare
>   Joshua 7)

And in Jesus' teaching, covetousness leads to a tormenting anxiety:

> "Teacher, tell my brother to divide the family inheritance with me."…And he said to them, "Take care! Be on your guard against all kinds of greed; for one's life does not consist in the abundance of possessions."…He said to his disciples, "Therefore I tell you, do not worry about your life, what you will eat, or about your body, what you will wear." (Luke 12:13, 15, 22; compare Acts 5:1–14)

Thus, in creation, the forces of chaos are opposed by God's powerful will *for orderly fruitfulness*. In historic community, the forces of injustice and exploitation are opposed by God's will for *responsible, equitable justice*, which yields security. In personal existence, driven, anxious self-seeking is opposed by God's will for *generous caring*. The biblical vision of *shalom* functions always as a firm rejection of values and lifestyles that seek security and well-being in manipulative ways at the expense of another part of creation, another part of the community, or a brother or sister. The vision of the biblical way affirms that communal well-being comes by living God's dream, not by idolatrous self-aggrandizement. The alternative is to so distort creation as never to know what it means to celebrate the Sabbath. Either we strive to secure our own existence or we celebrate the joy and rest of Sabbath, knowing that God has already secured it for us. *Shalom* is received by grateful creation.

Maintaining the Vision

The Bible is not romantic about its vision. It never assumes *shalom* will come naturally or automatically. Indeed, there are many ways of compromising God's will for *shalom*.

One way the community can say no to the vision and live without *shalom* is to deceive itself into thinking that its *private arrangements* of injustice and exploitation are suitable ways of living:

For from the least to the greatest of them,
every one is greedy for unjust gain;
and from prophet to priest,
every one deals falsely.
They have healed the wound of my people lightly,
saying, *"Shalom, shalom,"* when there is no *shalom*.
(Jeremiah 6:13–14, author's translation; compare
Ezekiel 13:10, 16 and Amos 6:1–6)

Shalom in a special way is the task and burden of the well-off and powerful. They are the ones held accountable for *shalom*. The prophets persistently criticized and polemicized against those well-off and powerful ones who legitimized their selfish prosperity and deceived themselves into thinking it was permanent. The prophetic vision of *shalom* stands against all private arrangements, all "separate peaces," all ghettos that pretend the others are not there (compare Luke 16:

19–31). Religious legitimacy in the service of self-deceiving well-being is a form of chaos. *Shalom* is never the private property of the few.[4]

A second way of perverting the vision is to take a *short-term view.* Isaiah preserves a story of King Hezekiah, who bargained the future of his people for present accommodation. He is condemned for thinking: "'There will be peace *(shalom)* and security in my days'" (Isaiah 39:8). A moment of well-being can be had today with enormous charges made against tomorrow. Parents pile up debts of hatred and abuse for their children to pay off. But the prophet is clear. *Shalom* is never short-range; eventually, someone must pay dearly. Caring for creation is never a one-generation deal (see Jeremiah 31:29–30; Ezekiel 18:2).

A third way of abusing God's will for *shalom* is to *credit certain props* as sources of life—for example, to idolize political or religious furniture and pretend it is the power of God. Jeremiah saw that his people regarded the temple as a way of *shalom,* apparently thinking it was available and cheap without regard to demands that came with the package (Jeremiah 7:1–10). Similarly, Jesus exposed a self-deceiving mentality that valued particular moral rules at the expense of persons (Matthew 15:1–20). The vision of *shalom* is so great that it would be nice to manage and control it—to know the formula that puts it at our disposal—either by a religion of piety or morality or by a technology that puts it on call (see Deuteronomy 18:9–14). But *shalom* is not subject to our best knowledge or our cleverest gimmicks. It comes only through the costly way of caring.

A Vital Hope

Shalom is an enduring vision. It is promised persistently and hoped for always. But there are those occasions when it is an especially vital hope. One such time was during Israel's exile. Among the eloquent spokesmen for the vision in that period was Jeremiah. And among the most extraordinary texts is this letter he wrote to the exiles urging the validity of the vision even among displaced persons:

I will fulfill to you my promise and bring you back to this place. For surely I know the plans I have for you, says the LORD, plans for your welfare *(shalom)* and not for harm, to

---

[4]Cf. Walter Brueggemann, *Finally Comes the Poet: Daring Speech for Proclamation* (Minneapolis: Fortress Press, 1989), 16.

give you a future with hope…When you search for me, you
will find me; if you seek me with all your heart, I will let you
find me, says the LORD, and I will restore your fortunes.
(Jeremiah 29:10–11, 13–14a)

On the face of it, the text is simply a promise that the exile will
eventually end. But the structure moves from promise (verse 10) to
land (place, verse 14). So again Israel is set on that joyous, tortuous
path from promise to land, from wandering to security, from chaos to
shalom. Thus, the experience of exile—like every experience—gets
read as a part of the pilgrimage of this incredible vision of God with
the people of Israel.

In a letter to the exiles in Babylon, Jeremiah uses our term twice.
Jeremiah 29:11 has the affirmation that God wills *shalom* even for the
exiles. God does not will evil, even though exile feels like evil. God
wills a future and a hope—a promise thrusting to reality. We take the
affirmation routinely. But its boldness can surprise when it is spoken
in a time of despair and cynicism, when "the center cannot hold,"
when everything has collapsed and everyone is weary, with hope
exhausted. At the root of history is the One who wills *shalom.* At its
end is the One who calls us to *shalom,* secure community, a golden
calf that frequently seems to be against all the stubborn facts. A lesser
resource will scarcely refute despair or enable alienated ones to care.
Only being grasped by the Holy One will do this—the One who
dares to promise and dream when the rest of us have given up.

And what does Jeremiah mean? Simply that God is there. We are
not abandoned. (Note the affirmation in exilic texts, Isaiah 41:10,
14; 43:1–2, 5; 49:14–15; 54:7–10 and, in a quite different context,
Matthew 28:20.) We are heard by God, who also answers (Exodus
3:7ff.; Isaiah 65:24). Ours is not an empty world of machinery where
we get what we have coming to us. No! Caring, healing communication
is still possible. There is this *Thou* who calls every historical *I* to
community. Life is not a driven or an anxious monologue. The Lord
is findable, which is a gospel theme of great importance when God
seems dead or hidden (see Deuteronomy 4:29–31; Isaiah 55:6, both
texts from the exile). The vision of *shalom* is most eloquently expressed
in times very much like our own, when resources for faith to endure
are hardly available. Thus, for example, in Isaiah 65:21, *shalom* motifs
come together; in 65:25, reconciled creation; in 65:24, assured

dialogue.[5] It is natural that the question of *shalom* should vex the church precisely when life seems so much a monologue.

The other use of *shalom* in Jeremiah's letter to the exiles is in 29:7:

> But seek the *shalom* of the city where I have sent you into exile, and pray to the LORD on its behalf, for in its *shalom* you will find your *shalom*. (author's translation)

Imagine that! A letter written to displaced persons in hated Babylon, where they have gone against their will and watched their life and culture collapse. And they are still there, yearning to go home, despising their captors and resenting their God—if, indeed, God is still their God. And the speaker for the vision dares to say, "Your *shalom* will be found in Babylon's *shalom*." The well-being of the chosen ones is tied to the well-being of that hated metropolis, which the chosen people fear and resent. It is profound and disturbing to discover that this remarkable religious vision will have to be actualized in the civil community. The stuff of well-being is the sordid collection of rulers, soldiers, wardens, and carpetbaggers in Judah and in every place of displaced, exhausted hope. It is an incredible vision even now for people of faith who feel pressed and angry about the urban shape of our existence, to say nothing about the urban shape of our vision. But again it is affirmed that God's *shalom* is known only by those in inclusive, caring community.

The letter of Jeremiah to the displaced persons surely did not meet expectations. No doubt they hoped for a purer gospel, a neater promise, a distinctive future. But God's exiles are always learning the hard way that the thrust toward viable unity must find a way to include the very ones we prefer to exclude. Depending on how deep the hatred and how great the fear, this promise of *shalom* with hated Babylon is a glorious promise or a sobering thought; but it is our best vision, a vision always rooted in and addressed to historical realities.[6]

The Embodiment of *Shalom*

The only *shalom* promised is one in the midst of historical reality, which comes close to saying "incarnation." The only God we know

---

[5]Cf. Brueggemann, *Theology of the Old Testament,* 548–49.
[6]Cf. Brueggemann, *Finally Comes the Poet,* 37–41.

entered history, appeared as a person. *Shalom* of a biblical kind is always somewhat scandalous—never simply a liturgical experience or a mythical statement, but one facing our deepest divisions and countering with a vision.

The Pauline letters speak of this. There seem to be so many categories and divisions and discriminating marks that separate and pigeonhole, but there is also this:

> There is no longer Jew or Greek, there is no longer slave or free, there is no longer male and female; for all of you are one in Christ Jesus. And if you belong to Christ, then you are Abraham's offspring, heirs according to the promise. (Galatians 3:28–29)

Called to the Lord's single community, bearers of God's single promise, children of the one Abraham. Paul runs blatantly over our favorite divisions—black-white, rich-poor, male-female, East-West, old-young, or whatever—finding them unreal and uninteresting. Those factors count not at all—our anxiety, drivenness, covetousness, injustice, chaos—none of these ever secures our existence. Yet we are secure, called to *shalom* from all our desperate efforts at security and our foolish manipulations to ensure dominance. Then Paul comes right out and says it ever more flatly: "He [Jesus] is our peace *(shalom)*" (Ephesians 2:14).

He got the lepers and the Pharisees all together again, the sons of Isaac and the heirs of Hagar, or so the vision lets us hope. He is known in the breaking of bread; he is crucified and risen; he is coming again— he who draws all people to himself, who rose from the dead and defied the governor, but who could not save himself. We say he embodies our vision and empowers us to live it.

We are sometimes children of the eighth day. And we risk an embracing of the vision. It is remarkable that lions and lambs share fodder, that widows and people of means have a common heritage, that our future is not in compulsive drivenness but in free caring. That vision surrounds us and addresses us, but we see only in a glass darkly.

2

SHALOM FOR "HAVES" AND "HAVE-NOTS"

Then the LORD said, "I have observed the misery of my people who are in Egypt; I have heard their cry on account of their taskmasters. Indeed, I know their sufferings, and I have come down to deliver them from the Egyptians, and to bring them up out of that land to a good and broad land, a land flowing with milk and honey, to the country of the Canaanites, the Hittites, the Amorites, the Perizzites, the Hivites, and the Jebusites."

EXODUS 3:7–8

Judah and Israel were as numerous as the sand by the sea; they ate and drank and were happy.

1 KINGS 4:20

Shalom can mean many things. But what we take it to mean is not accidental. The way we define it makes sense in the context of our lives. We define the word and use it—as we do all words—as a bearer of peculiar meanings that match up with our needs, hopes, fears, and visions. And the context in which we set the word *shalom* will make a difference in how it comes through to us and what freight we assign to it.

I shall begin with contrasting two contexts in which biblical faith most likely was articulated. I will want to suggest that in each of these contexts, the term *shalom* has very different nuances attached to it.

Shalom for "Have-Nots"

First, let me report on the Moses-Joshua-Samuel prophetic tradition. This is the one we know best and the one most of us discern as "normative" for the Bible. I will not here review all the critical judgments behind my reasoning, but will simply state that this is the material in the Old Testament that is popularly labeled and dismissed as "deuteronomic." I suggest that this mind-set—and, therefore, the literature—emerged from a situation of "have-nots" working with the question of survival. We may talk of the people behind the literature as the slave people led by Moses or as the Joshua-Samuel-Judges people who were an unwelcome presence in a Canaanite-Philistine context where they had only the poor land and could barely survive. Or we may go to the other end of that historical sequence (as many scholars do) and locate the final form of that literature in the sixth century B.C.E. exile. Either way, the people who shaped this literature were interested in the question of survival—either actual physical, historical survival, or at least the survival of faith and meaning. They lived their lives aware of the acute precariousness of their situation.

People who live in the midst of precariousness shape their vocabulary and their faith, their perceptions and their liturgy, in a distinctive way. One of the most important ways the Israelites expressed their faith was around the theme of "cry out, hear, and deliver."[1] Their form of faith was to cry out. God's form of presence and graciousness was to hear their cry, be moved by it, and act to deliver them from the trouble in which they found themselves. Claus Westermann has said, "The cry out of the depths is the starting point of the event."[2]

---

[1]See the discussion of Walter Brueggemann, "From Hurt to Joy, From Death to Life," *Interpretation* 28 (1974): 3–19; and Claus Westermann, "The Role of the Lament in the Theology of the Old Testament," *Interpretation* 28 (1974): 20–38.
[2]Westermann, "Role of the Lament."

This "cry out, hear, and deliver" way of expression is established early in the faith tradition, as early as the exodus:[3]

> The Israelites groaned under their slavery, and cried out. Out of the slavery their cry for help rose up to God. God heard their groaning, and God remembered his covenant with Abraham, Isaac, and Jacob. God looked upon the Israelites, and God took notice of them.
>
> Then the LORD said, "I have observed the misery of my people who are in Egypt; I have heard their cry on account of their taskmasters. Indeed, I know their sufferings, and I have come down to deliver them." (Exodus 2:23–25; 3:7–8a)

The key words are *cried out* and *deliver (za'aq/yatsa')*. Israel is a people who cry out. Yahweh is a God who saves. That is the form in which the covenant is expressed. In crying out, Israel expresses total dependence upon God. In saving, Yahweh manifests complete fidelity to Israel. Later in the same narrative, though probably from another source is the following:

> "I have also heard the *groaning* of the Israelites whom the Egyptians are holding as slaves, and I have remembered my covenant...I will free you from the burdens of the Egyptians and *deliver* you from slavery to them. I will *redeem* you." (Exodus 6:5–6)

And it is not different in the later expressions of a similar perception. It is clear in the narratives of Judges:

> He *delivered* them from the hand of their enemies all the days of the judge; for the LORD would be moved to pity by their *groaning* because of those who persecuted and oppressed them. (Judges 2:18b)

And the same structure is put to Israel by Yahweh with heavy sarcasm, following an affirming:

> "You *cried* to me, and I *delivered* you out of their hand...Go and *cry* to the gods whom you have chosen; let them *deliver* you in the time of your distress." (Judges 10:12b, 14)

---

[3]Cf. Walter Brueggemann, *Old Testament Theology: Essays on Structure, Theme, and Text,* ed. Patrick D. Miller (Minneapolis: Fortress Press, 1992), 47.

And even as the period of precariousness moved toward its royal end, the same structure is apparent in the work of Samuel:

"Do not cease to *cry out* to the LORD our God for us, and pray that he may *save* us from the hand of the Philistines."…Samuel *cried out* to the LORD for Israel, and the LORD *answered* him. (1 Samuel 7:8–9)

Clearly this is not simply one among many alternative ways of speaking. It is the characteristic way in which the children of Israel spoke, and undoubtedly the way they perceived reality. How could it be otherwise? Clearly life was precarious, and they reflected on where they needed help for survival. And the conclusion is a *theology of salvation*. This theology is one of needy, helpless folk who sometimes cry to Yahweh and *are* rescued, but who sometimes do not, and suffer for it. Their notion of God is one who will intervene and save, but who first must be addressed in trust. Their notion of themselves is that of a dependent people crying out for a vision of survival and salvation. *Precarious people bent on survival visualize God as a strong, masculine, transforming intruder.*

Shalom for "Haves"

There is a second distinct alternative in the Old Testament traditions, which provides us with a very different way of doing theology, a different meaning for *shalom,* and a different way of perceiving the world and trusting God. My impression is that our normative theology has been formulated in a situation of precariousness concerned with survival. But there is a set of traditions that has little sense of precariousness and is not much worried about survival. These traditions cluster around Noah-Abraham-David. In broad, sweeping terms I propose that these traditions emerge from and reflect a situation of "haves" whose life is not precarious and who are concerned with questions of *proper management and joyous celebration.* It is the well-off who can reflect on proper management, who are aware that blessings have been given to them that must be wisely cared for and properly maintained for the generations to come. It is the well-off who can be reflective enough to care intentionally about the joyous celebration of life.

My point here is a simple but nonetheless important one. People who are well-off have very different perceptions of life and a very different theological agenda from those who must worry about survival. Both are in the Bible, and while church theology has taken the *Bible's theology of survival* seriously, it has been less perceptive about the *Bible's theology of management and celebration.* This theology of well-being seems to be a product of periods of prosperity and security—very likely the product of royal achievement. Thus, it probably has its natural setting in the environs of the king—precisely the one with a world to manage and with cause for rejoicing. Claus Westermann more than anyone has helped me distinguish this theology from that of salvation. Whereas the traditions we have previously considered are concerned with salvation, this theology is concerned with blessing:

> Besides the polar works of saving and judging, the Old Testament knows a wholly different kind of divine acting in history: a constant acting not manifested in momentary events, namely God's work of blessing. Blessing really means the power of fertility. God's blessing causes a development in and growing, a ripening and fruitbearing, a silent advance of the power of life in all realms.[4]

In what follows, Westermann locates this kind of reflection especially in the patriarchal narratives, the reflections on the land and the stories of kingship and temple. He asserts:

> This term [salvation history] blurs the *difference* between God's work of salvation and his work of blessing…This history cannot be reduced to a single concept, certainly not to the concept of salvation history.[5]

Thus, a theology of blessing for the well-off "haves" is very different from a theology of salvation for the precarious "have-nots." Obviously the well-off do not expect their faith to begin in a cry, but rather, in a song. They do not expect or need intrusion, but they rejoice in stability. They do not crave an upheaval—a discontinuity—such as a "mighty saving deed," but they celebrate the solidarity of continuity, which means the durability of a world and a social order that have been beneficial to them. Predictably, such a way of perceiving the world and responding in faith requires a very different rhetoric.

---

[4]Claus Westermann, "Creation and History in the Old Testament," in *The Gospel and Human Destiny,* ed. Vilmos Vajta (Minneapolis: Augsburg, 1971), 30.
[5]Ibid., 32.

Unfortunately, Old Testament scholarship has concentrated on the salvation history and Mosaic covenant aspects of the Old Testament. This is reflected in the credo studies of Gerhard von Rad, and in George Ernest Wright's emphasis on the mighty acts of God. So we are only at the beginning in locating the elements in the rhetoric of blessing. The focus is not an urgent petition for intrusion into human affairs, but a settled, serene affirmation about the way the world is ordered. The following probably reflect such a worldview:

It was very good. (Genesis 1:31)

"As long as the earth endures, seedtime and harvest, cold and heat, summer and winter, day and night, shall not cease." (Genesis 8:22)

"Even though you intended to do harm to me, God intended it for good, in order to preserve a numerous people, as he is doing today." (Genesis 50:20)

I will make for you a great name, like the name of the great ones of the earth. (2 Samuel 7:9)

But I will not take my steadfast love from him...Your house and your kingdom shall be made sure forever before me; your throne shall be established forever. (2 Samuel 7:15–16)

She bore a son, and he named him Solomon. The LORD loved him. (2 Samuel 12:24)

Judah and Israel were as numerous as the sand by the sea; they ate and drank and were happy. (1 Kings 4:20)

The eternal God is your dwelling place, and underneath are the everlasting arms. (Deuteronomy 33:27, RSV; compare Psalm 90:1–2.)

There is great variety in these statements, which are not all of the same kind, but several things are to be noted. First, they are extremely positive and confident. Second, they are not dialogical. They don't speak to anybody and expect a response, the opposite of the "cry-save" pattern we have seen. Third, they recognize that things are good, and they yearn for maintenance of the status quo; they do not expect, need, or desire an intrusion. They await only assurance and reassurance that the world as they know it and *possess* it will be maintained. People who have access to the good life do not await gifts. They only celebrate the gifts already given and seek to preserve them. In some circles, this contrast of salvation for the "have-nots" and blessing for the "haves" may be characterized as the tension of "already" and "not yet." Those who have, *already* have it. For them the world is already healthy and whole. For those deprived—who await God's intrusion—they have it *not yet,* and their perceptions are the desperate/hopeful waiting that what is not yet will soon be.

This *theology of proper management and joyous celebration* occurs in several kinds of texts, which have been neglected in most church usage. Following are some of these texts:

- The creation traditions, which focus on the enduring structure of creation, expressed as we have seen in Genesis 1:31 and Genesis 8:22, but also in many psalms.
- The wisdom texts, which, as von Rad has shown, are concerned with the interconnectedness of things.[6] It is affirmed that the world does indeed hang together, that there is linkage between how we live and what we get. It is this that lies behind much of the wisdom teaching recently presented by Koch as a "sphere of automatic deed-consequence experience."[7] Worth noting is Robert Gordis' shrewd assessment of the sociology of wisdom: "It is the thesis of this paper that Wisdom Literature…was fundamentally the product of the upper classes in society, who lived principally in the capital, Jerusalem…As is to be expected, the upper classes were conservative in their outlook, basically satisfied with the status quo and opposed to change."[8] Such a worldview is not self-seeking, though it can become that. It is,

---

[6]Gerhard von Rad, *Old Testament Theology* 1 (New York: Harper and Brothers, 1962), 418–29. See also von Rad, *Wisdom in Israel* (New York: Abingdon Press, 1972), 113–37.

[7]Klaus Koch, "Gibt es em Vergeltungsdogma im alten Testament?" *Zeitschrift für Theologie und Kirche* 52 (1955): 1–42, reprinted in *Um das Prinzip der Vergeltung in Religion und Recht des alten Testaments,* ed. Klaus Koch (Darmstadt: Wissenschaftliche Buchgesellschaft, 1972), 130–80.

[8]Robert Gordis, "The Social Background of Wisdom Literature," in *Poets, Prophets and Sages* (Bloomington, Ind.: Indiana University Press, 1971), 162.

rather, the honest report on the way the world has been experienced by well-off people.

* The royal texts narrate about kings who have enormous power to manage and adequate wherewithal to celebrate. There is the sense that the king and the royal household have much entrusted to them, and therefore, proper management is important. Indeed a case is made in the royal texts that it is the right conduct of the king, that is, his responsible management, that keeps the world coherent and productive.[9] (Obviously the temptation to hubris is ever present, but that should not obscure the positive affirmations that must be made.)

This is a worldview that is nearly inevitable among the well-off. How can they minimize or deny the richness of the present, or fail to thank God for it, or be concerned that it should be maintained? Such affirmations form an important dimension of biblical faith.

Now, my impression about myself and about my professional colleagues is that we feel most comfortable with a theology of survival, which is orientated to an awaited intervention, which speaks of the awfulness of the present, the burdens of it, and the desperate promise of the new age. Perhaps that is because of our theological education or because of the socioeconomic setting out of which clergy come. Whatever the reasons, that is what we know best to speak about, and it is the way we do our theology. Thus, I want to affirm simply that out of a socioeconomic setting of disadvantage comes the stuff of the radical gospel of liberation, and lots of us are committed to it. Support for the connection between precarious survival and radical liberation theology is to be found in the brilliant studies of Paul Hanson[10] concerning the origins of and, more contemporarily, in the liberation theologies out of Latin America.[11]

I wish in no way to diminish the power and centrality of this theological posture. But it is important for us to observe that this other theology of proper management and joyous celebration is also biblical. Moreover, it is likely in our cultural setting that this theology is more appropriate to lots of folks who are increasingly well-off. We

---

[9]Cf.Brueggemann, *Theology of the Old Testament,* 600–621.

[10]Paul Hanson, "Old Testament Apocalyptic Reexamined," *Interpretation* 25 (1971): 454–79.

[11]See the bibliography of Robert McAfee Brown, *Religion and Violence* (Philadelphia: Westminster Press, 1973), 111–13.

should face that, professionally, it is harder to preach. It does not evoke the rhetoric of proclamation. Surely it has less bite to it, and it is more open to cultural accommodation.

The Polarity of *Shalom*

Now, I am not urging one worldview or the other. My topic is *shalom*. I am suggesting that there is ample evidence in the Bible for two very different views of *shalom* that can be found in the text, and it is important for us to locate the place where we make contact with the Bible. Or, put more sharply, it is important to locate the particular gospel we are preaching and to be sensitive to the proximate causes for our attraction to that formulation. If we are sensitive to the sociopolitical-economic factors in our theology, we may be more perceptive about what we mean when we use the word *shalom*—of course, always with good biblical authority

Our understanding of *shalom* invites us to share in the fundamental social polarity of the Bible. To recapitulate:

There is the tradition of the "have-nots" concerned with survival. That tradition may be located especially in the prophets, as heirs of Moses. Their mood is always to declare the end of the old, to make radical announcements of God's newness, and to make radical demands for new obedience. They focus on the sharp discontinuity between the way it has been and the way it now is, or is to be, because of God's action. As Hanson has shown, this radical orientation toward newness—both new gift and new demand—issues in apocalyptic. And if Hanson is correct, apocalyptic is the traditional rejection of the unbearable old for the sake of what is yet to be. That is a tradition that surely points toward Jesus with his radical announcement of the new age and the new kingdom.

Alongside this is the biblical tradition of the "haves" who value their many resources. This tradition may be located especially in the circles around the kings-persons entrusted with much who are prepared to care wisely for the maintenance of blessings and the prudent utilization of resources. This tradition, I suggest, is reflected in the wisdom teachers and, subsequently, the rabbis. They are the people who care so much for the way the world is that they devote primary energies into ordering what has been entrusted to us. So they care a great deal about the costs and benefits of alternative ways to manage resources. They do not await a new age because the present age—that is, the present arrangement—already has within it the forces of creativity and generativity.

In this dual context we may speak of *shalom*. My impression is that the introduction of the *shalom* emphasis in the church was to stress the possibility of the new age in a radical way. But that poses two kinds of problems for us. First, a strong case can be made that *shalom* in the Bible is closer to blessing than to salvation—closer to valuing a prosperous, beneficial order than to the radical expectation of a new one. It is, of course, possible to reinterpret the symbols another way, but when we do it, we should know that that is what we are about. Second, and perhaps more crucial, my impression of the constituency of the average church is that we are by and large a "blessed" people. We are not the deprived, the "have-nots." We are typically middle-class American, which means that our life is not terribly precarious even though we have our anxieties. Now, if the Bible maintains the poles of the issue, and if our constituency is as I have suggested, that poses hard questions about how we shall speak of *shalom*. Shall we speak of it in terms of yearning precariousness or grateful complacency? Shall we focus on "already" or "not yet"? Shall we stress a new future or the maintenance of what is?

I have the impression that a case can be made that Jesus practiced both of these. With Ernst Käsemann,[12] we can say that Jesus is informed by apocalyptic, and surely the Qumran evidence suggests a perception of reality congenial to the "have-nots." There is no doubt that among the "wretched of the earth" he found his natural constituency, and to them he offered a gospel of liberation and the hope of a transformed world. But one can also argue with Davies[13] that Jesus knew and valued the traditions of the wise and the rabbis and that he spoke also to the "haves" about their responsibility and accountability. He spoke about the interconnectedness of life and the need for management of the

---

[12]Ernst Käsemann, *Essays on New Testament Themes* (London: SCM Press, 1964); see the reports of Klaus Koch, *The Rediscovery of Apocalyptic* (Naperville, Ill.: Alec R. Allenson, 1972) and Carl Braaten, *Christ and Counter-Culture: Apocalyptic Themes in Theology and Culture* (Philadelphia: Fortress Press, 1972), 2–23. Hanson, *Dawn of Apocalyptic,* 479, refers to world-weariness, in connection with the sociological context of apocalyptic. The theme is pertinent to us because world-weariness is a pervasive concern among us.

[13]W. D. Davies, *The Sermon on the Mount* (Cambridge: Cambridge University Press, 1966); *The Setting of the Sermon on the Mount* (Cambridge: Cambridge University Press, 1964); and his entire approach to Jesus through a rabbinic context.

gifts presented to us. He apparently moved back and forth in this polarity, having a variety of ways of speaking in various contexts.

Those are some options before us as we work with the *shalom* idea. I think we have not begun to think seriously about the socioeconomic-political dimensions of our faith and our theology. I don't believe there is a single correct answer about where to locate ourselves on the polarity of precariousness and well-being, and I don't propose that we should give answers. But we do well to be alert to the polarity and the direct connection between our theology and our placement in life.

- So we image the *world* either as a dreaded burden soon to pass away or as a rich gift to be valued and nurtured.
- So we image ourselves as *persons* either as among the wretched, waiting for a new deal, or as a trusted, valued manager prepared to act responsibly and confidently.
- So we image and preach *the good news* either as a promise of the upheaval or as an assurance of the durability of what is.

We have work to do to locate our gospel and our tilt as persons. Of course, I am being simplistic by suggesting only the two poles. We move in and out of the polarity. We don't need to be at one extreme or the other, and persons are located at many points on the continuum. But we are by and large unaware of where we and where our institutions are, and then we are vulnerable to the assignments made to us by society and even by our own special constituency.

Two Models of *Shalom*

Related to the two poles of perception described above are two important models of *shalom*. For the precarious, *shalom* can be understood as the assurance that there is a hearer for our cries, an intruder and intervener who comes to transform our lives. For the well-off, *shalom* can be understood as buoyant confidence that the world will hold together because there is a maintainer and embracer who abides and who certifies our existence in the face of all its disintegration. *Shalom* is not what we have to do; it is a gift from the intruding transformer and the certifying maintainer. Israel can say both "He comes," and "Underneath are the everlasting arms." They are both statements about the one who is as father and mother to us—as father who intrudes, as mother who embraces. And we are recipients of the gift of *shalom*.

The world does not know that. The world believes there is only us, only our work, our attainments, our anxieties, our successes, and our failures. We can image this other dispenser of *shalom*. We know the transformation and the buoyancy that come to us in spite of ourselves because of this other one. Amazing as it is, we know the name of that other one, and this fact is at the center of the *shalom* given to us.

PART TWO

A Vision of Freedom

3

SHALOM AS FREEDOM AND UNITY

Remember that you were at that time without Christ, being aliens from the commonwealth of Israel, and strangers to the covenants of promise, having no hope and without God in the world. But now in Christ Jesus you who once were far off have been brought near by the blood of Christ. For he is our peace; in his flesh he has made both groups into one and has broken down the dividing wall, that is, the hostility between us. He has abolished the law with its commandments and ordinances, that he might create in himself one new humanity in place of the two, thus making peace, and might reconcile both groups to God in one body through the cross, thus putting to death that hostility through it. So he came and proclaimed peace to you who were far off and peace to those who were near; for through him both of us have access in one Spirit to the Father. So then you are no longer strangers and aliens, but you are citizens with the saints and also members of the household of God, built upon the foundation of the apostles and prophets, with Christ Jesus himself as the cornerstone. In him the whole structure is joined together and grows into a holy temple in the Lord; in whom you also are built together spiritually into a dwelling place for God.

EPHESIANS 2:12–22

39

Shalom is a tricky idea because it permits so many variant meanings to be assigned to it. But for all the possible variants, the word and notion of *shalom* has a radical nuance in our church context. It is an announcement that God has a vision of how the world shall be and is not yet. And the faith affirmed in the church is the twin resolve that we mean to discern God's vision of what the world shall be and that we mean to live toward that vision. Now, this resolve poses problems, because we are of two minds about it: (a) We really do choose to be charged and transformed by the gospel for God's new age, or (b) we resist, and refuse to change with all the energy and stamina we can muster. And that is very tricky, because we are radically concerned both to change and not to change. Moreover, I can think of many important ways in which *you* ought to change, and I can map it all out for you; but I do not want it to touch *me* so powerfully. So that is where we are and how we must be the church. It seems clear to me that at the same time we must be very bold about the claims of the gospel on the church, and very patient with one another as we hassle about change and the refusal to change.

No matter how much we resist specific claims implied in the notion of *shalom,* some things are clear:

- We are expected to go where we are not.
- We are expected to become who we are not.

God envisions church and world as they currently are not. But our job here is to put some substance to those claims. Surely *shalom* is like one of our well-known beers. When you've said *shalom,* "you've said it all." You've said "safe," "free," whole," "secure," "prosperous," "just," and on and on. So we say it all, but when we say it all, we run the risk of not saying anything compelling or clear. Therefore, let me suggest two word pairs that will add some freight to the word. I am aware that as soon as one does this, the cards are stacked in a certain direction. We do that all the time when we talk about scripture—and obviously scripture is our helpless victim, permitting the cards to be stacked in all sorts of directions—so I will boldly go in one direction.

I begin with a theme that was a lead theme for the 1975 World Council of Churches Assembly in Nairobi, Kenya: "Jesus Christ Frees and Unites."[1] That theme, which was articulated under the influence of theologian Jürgen Moltmann, is a good way to talk about *shalom,*

---

[1] See the pamphlet *Jesus Christ Frees and Unites* (New York: Friendship Press, 1974), prepared in anticipation of the 1975 meeting of the World Council of Churches in Nairobi, Kenya.

which among other things concerns freedom and unity. So let us take them one at a time.

Freedom

First, freedom. Jesus Christ frees. God intends freedom. It is clear to us all that our biblical story—our biblical faith—begins in the story of the exodus. Taken historically, that story is about how a band of Israelites were freed one wondrous night long ago. Taken theologically, it is the announcement of how God's purpose for freedom intruded radically into history and redesigned the direction of history. Now history becomes the story of how God's purpose for freedom made its powerful way in the affairs of persons and nations. Exodus has given us a model to understand that the key problem in human experience is the problem of oppression, embodied here in the Pharaoh. And the Passover, our memorial activity of the exodus, centers in the affirmation, "Once we were slaves and now we are free." It would be hard to imagine a bolder, more incredible, more difficult to understand, yet more precious memory than that. "Once we were slaves and now we are free." Israel first, and then the church, has reflected on that reality for a very long time, and the *shalom* emphasis in the church today invites us to fresh reflection: What is it that makes us free? What are the demands placed on us so that we can keep our freedom? In what ways could we lose our freedom?

There is something hidden and mysterious about freedom. It is like manna in that it is always a gift given, never a product controlled and understood. Like manna, it is not something that can be stored up and taken for granted, because then it turns sour and we don't have it anymore. It states the heart of our faith and our greatest temptation. It is that which we most want, and yet every calculating effort to secure it is fraught with problems. It is always a delicate reality in our lives. Freedom, when it comes, comes from God; yet at the same time those who do not care for, nurture, and celebrate freedom when it is given are likely not to enjoy it very long.

The theme is not different with Jesus, is it? Indeed, Ernst Käsemann, a German New Testament scholar, has a little book entitled *Jesus Means Freedom.*[2] That is precisely what Jesus meant then and means now. And that is why his coming is so glorious and so terrifying. The gospel stories about Jesus portray him as the one who went around

---

[2]Ernst Käsemann, *Jesus Means Freedom* (Philadelphia: Fortress Press, 1970).

causing exoduses in people's lives, and he did it as did God in the Israelite exodus—powerfully and dramatically, yet in hidden ways that few understood. The gospel stories may indeed be seen as a new exodus recital, for time after time Jesus led people out of old, secure oppressions into new wildernesses of freedom. To those enslaved by hunger, he gave the freedom of food, and even envisioned the new kingdom as a great banquet. To the guilt-ridden, he announced forgiveness, and they asked, "Where does he get authority to do this?" He came to lepers who had been excommunicated for their disease, and he freed them to come back into the beloved community, where all the resources for well-being were stored up for those who had entry. He came to a deaf man who could not communicate at all, and he opened his ears and empowered his tongue. And their reaction was predictable: "He has done everything well; he even makes the deaf to hear and the mute to speak" (Mark 7:37). When he dealt with the blindness of a man, all the fearful people and the experts—the fearful people and the experts are often the same folks—tried to make something bad out of it, but the blind man answered simply: "One thing I do know, that though I was blind, now I see" (John 9:25).

And the holy people said it was a shame. But how can you argue with it?

Looking at all these exodus stories, we do not know how people become enslaved. There isn't much here on how people lose their sight or their hearing or their speech. But when we *are* in slavery, we know we are there, unless we enjoy deceiving ourselves. And for that matter, the tellers of these stories, like those of the exodus of Israel, were reluctant to speculate on what causes freedom or how it happens. They knew only that the Lord intervened; and when the Lord came, things were changed, situations were reversed, lives were transformed, and communities were renewed.

The antitheses of freedom are all around us. We all know about the injustices in our society to all kinds of minority groups. And we all know about the personal and interpersonal claims we have that keep us from being free. We all know about the material lacks of people that keep them immobilized, and we know about the burdens of guilt and weariness that tie us up in knots. The common factor in all this is coercion—that we are driven, controlled, manipulated people, and we spend our lives doing what we must and what we do not choose. But Jesus, like God among the Israelites, is the powerful announcement that we do not need to live coerced lives. What a glory! Nobody understood this more than Paul, who had lived a coerced life until Jesus came into his life. Then the knot left the pit of his stomach, and he no longer needed to live in a frightened, safe, fetal position. So he asserts:

> For freedom Christ has set us free. Stand firm, therefore, and do not submit again to a yoke of slavery...For you were called to freedom, brothers and sisters. (Galatians 5:1, 13)

Obviously the freedom Paul discovered in the gospel was not an invitation to irresponsibility, nor was it a promise that there would be no more burdens or hardships. But now they are the responsibilities, burdens, and hardships of a free person, one not driven, but one facing options and having the power to choose the good news against all the bad forms of news that make promises that can never be kept.

Slavery is many different things. We must take care that we do not drive a wedge between people who are physically poor and deprived and so suffer, and people who have lots of "stuff" but still do not live free lives. We must not pit against each other sociological and psychological forms of slavery—either saying they are the same or arguing that one is deeper and hurts more than another. Whatever the slavery that binds a person, that is the one that counts. Let us characterize slavery simply as that which keeps us from being joyous. When we locate that, we shall be close to the source of our oppression. I have tried to reflect on the things that preclude joy. They include at least these: fear, a feeling of worthlessness, a lack of food, a lack of love, devotion to phony loyalties, and frantic, nonproductive obligations. You can continue the list as it touches your life, but they are all things that keep us coerced as though we always serve the company store, and so we do not rejoice. As church folks, we would do well to reflect on the kinds of enslavement in our church and in our community. The agents of enslavement are the enemies of the gospel, and though we need to be concerned with large public issues, the forces of coercion are also very near to us. It would be suggestive and healthy to think of such factors in our midst and then to explore what it would be like to build a parish budget and design a parish program to address the agents of slavery among us.

Paul reflected a long time on slavery and freedom. He did not think there are a lot of little slaveries, but that they are all of a piece, and we can name them. He called them "elemental spirits":

We were enslaved to the *elemental spirits* of the world. (Galatians 4:3)

If with Christ you died to the *elemental spirits* of the universe, why do you live as if you still belonged to the world? (Colossians 2:20)

This may sound primitive today because most people do not believe that way. But even if we are more sophisticated, we still know that the powers that coerce us are powerful and alive, and for some reason we are not free to live our lives toward joy. We spend our time crying, satisfying others, measuring up, meeting quotas.

If "elemental spirits" is problematic for you, try thinking about the pictures in your head of yourself, of the world, and of God. Jesus is the one who has offered us alternative pictures of how we understand, share in, and relate to the world. They are, after the language of the old hymn, "wonderful pictures of life." He wills us not to honor all those coercions anymore because they have no real power and no legitimate authority in our lives. They have only the power and legitimacy we give them, and that is self-deception.

Unity

The second component of our theme is "Jesus unites." God wills unity. God wants folks to be together. God is against estrangement and fragmentation. Whereas most of the freedom texts are rooted in the Moses events, it is curious and worth noting that the unity texts are to be found for the most part in the texts related to the Abraham tradition. It is the Abraham tradition that announces the great vision of unity. It is here that Israel is announced as the source of blessing for all the peoples. As Hans Walter Wolff has shown, the entire emphasis of the old Genesis tradition is that this blessing should be an ordering to bring harmony to all the elements of that world.[3] The idea of a divided, hostile, noncommunicative world is not willed by God, but is indeed the result of seeking to secure existence on grounds other than the gospel. (Compare Genesis 11:1–9.)

---

[3]Hans Walter Wolff, "The Kerygma of the Yahwist," *Interpretation* 20 (1966): 131–58.

It is especially in the tradition of Isaiah, which I take to be informed by the Abraham vision, that the will for unity comes to clear expression. In Isaiah 2:2–4, the poet offers a vision of Jerusalem as the place where all the variant and even discordant elements of life shall get together: "All the nations shall stream to it." The same passage portrays the beating of swords into plowshares and spears into pruning hooks. "Nation shall not lift up sword against nation, neither shall they learn war any more." That is not simply a vision of a political arrangement nor a disarmament program, but the emergence of a new world, a new situation in which people are able to trust and to communicate enough so that they no longer need to be armed. God wills for the world—for our world—a center of justice and righteousness that will get our minds off our petty agenda and our penchant to protect our little investments. I find that vision overwhelming—and not very welcome, because the things I value most I am reluctant to lose or risk, and even more reluctant to share.

And then there is this most majestic view of unity:

The wolf shall live with the lamb,
    the leopard shall lie down with the kid,
the calf and the lion and the fatling together,
    and a little child shall lead them.
The cow and the bear shall graze,
    their young shall lie down together;
    and the lion shall eat straw like the ox.
The nursing child shall play over the hole of the asp,
    and the weaned child shall put its hand on the adder's den.
    (Isaiah 11:6–8)

Unheard of and unimaginable! All these images of unity sound to me so abnormal that they are not worth reflecting on. But then I look again and notice something else. The poet means to say that in the new age, these are the normal things. And the effect of the poem is to expose the real abnormalities of life, which we have taken for granted. We have lived with things abnormal so long that we have gotten used to them and we think they are normal.[4] From our family,

---

[4]Marion J. Levy, Jr., *Modernization: Latecomers and Survivors* (New York: Basic Books, 1972), has addressed the problem of accepting the bizarre as normal: "The main source of the subversiveness of the patterns of modernization when they come in contact with non-modernized people inheres above all in the utter bizarreness of the everyday patterns that the highly modernized everywhere take so complacently for granted" (11). In speaking of education for the future and our modern expectations, he asserts, "One of the queerest things of all is that we take this unusual combination of characteristics so very much for granted" (137).

one of the abnormalities we take as normal is that father and sons quarrel about television: "Turn it off," "You're watching too much," and so on. That is just what we do in our family. Ask any one of us about the activity shared by father and sons, and we will all say, "We quarrel about TV; that is our indoor sport." But it is abnormal, isn't it?

There are other unquestioned abnormalities. We have taken it for granted that the United States is supposed to get into wars around the world and we do just that. We have always done it (which means for the last few decades), and we really can't imagine not doing it. Furthermore, we are insensitive to it. We are unaware of how abnormal and unnatural it all is. Or, closer to home, think of the abnormalities of interracial relations; too often, decades after the civil rights movement, the assumptions about other races and ethnicities linger on. It's too easy for "us" to assume that "they" are "just that way," or that people who live in "that part of town" or "that city" are all naturally the way they are. In cases from redlining to racial profiling, it still goes on. Not only does it not seem politically possible to have it otherwise, but it seems like the natural order of things, and we just let it go at that.

Consider, however, the vision of lions and lambs. We have long known that it is the business of lions to eat mutton and the business of lambs to stay where it is safe. Or that children and snakes are really "natural" enemies. But this vision is about another kind of reality in which natural enemies become playmates and friends and brothers and sisters. The vision for unity is radical and not to come without pain. But it is the pain of the good news, the announcement that God wills the world another way, and it will be that way.

The unity theme is not as prominent in Jesus' teaching as that of freedom, but it is there:

> "I lay down my life for the sheep. I have other sheep that do not belong to this fold. I must bring them also, and they will listen to my voice. So there will be one flock, one shepherd." (John 10:15b–16)

> "And I, when I am lifted up from the earth, will draw all people to myself." (John 12:32)

Jesus, even in the synoptic gospels, never acknowledges the neat divisions and separations made between leper and well person, between lawkeeper and sinner, between the good folks and the "others." He lived and acted as though there were one world for all the folks, and in his actions he created the new reality. It is significant that in both John 10 and 12, the vision of unity is through the pain of his death. There is dying that goes with unity. There is pain that goes with giving up swords and spears and living with pruning hooks and plows. There is pain and death and vulnerability that come with living in the world defenseless, but in that way comes unity.

Whereas the Jesus texts were much more about freedom, Paul reflects much on unity. The central text of most of our current thinking about *shalom* is in Ephesians. Paul writes:

> Remember that you were at that time without Christ, being aliens from the commonwealth of Israel, and strangers to the covenants of promise, having no hope and without God in the world. But now in Christ Jesus you who once were far off have been brought near by the blood of Christ. For he is our peace; in his flesh he has made both groups into one and has broken down the dividing wall, that is, the hostility between us. He has abolished the law with its commandments and ordinances, that he might create in himself one new humanity in place of the two, thus making peace. (Ephesians 2:12–15)

And in the same letter he concludes the opening lyric this way:

> He has made known to us the mystery of his will, according to his good pleasure that he set forth in Christ, as a plan for the fullness of time, to *gather up all things* in him, things in heaven and things on earth. (Ephesians 1:9–10)

And more specifically, he states the reality of unity, linking it precisely to the Abraham vision:

> There is no longer Jew or Greek, there is no longer slave or free, there is no longer male and female; for all of you are one in Christ Jesus. And if you belong to Christ, then you are Abraham's offspring, heirs according to the promise. (Galatians 3:28–29)

And then, of the texts from the Pauline tradition, this most eloquent one:

He himself is before all things, and in him all things hold together. (Colossians 1:17)

That was a radical statement in the first century, when all the splits and resentments in society were apparent and there seemed no way to overcome them. It was radical, given polytheism and religious pluralism. This tiny little community, in the face of large urban resistance, announced another vision of how the world really was to be. The world is not intended for alienation, but for unity!

The good news of unity is directed to the separated and the alienated. God aches at the disunity in the world. I want you to reflect on what kinds of things keep us at odds. Such factors include, at least, pride—of place and of accomplishments—greed for stuff and for power, fear, and misunderstanding. As I thought about this, it occurred to me that most obviously, fear is on the list as an agent of slavery and as an agent of separation. And surely in Jesus' ministry, everybody with whom he had to do—the well-off and the outcasts—everybody had an agenda of fears that immobilized and alienated. And it is not different now, is it? So again, it would be useful for church folks to make a list of the agents of separation in their community and parish and then to address those agents—through spending and through programming—to see how the church might serve God's will for unity in a world of fragmentation. Where are the crunches in your life? We know about some standard ones, those of old-young, rich-poor, black-white, conservative-liberal, male-female. In the church sometimes it is people–local leadership, or even our church's national offices. We won't run out of agendas to address. All that seems so natural to us, but it is against the purpose of God, and it is not the wave of the future.

Peter Berger et al., in the book *The Homeless Mind,* make a shrewd analysis of our modern mentality.[5] They discern that one of the things that permits the technological, bureaucratic world to function is our commitment to *componentiality*—their word for people and roles and ideas and everything else being seen as replaceable parts. Being only a component may be progress, but, as Berger et al. show, it is also most problematic. They do not suggest that componentiality is equivalent to fragmentation, but that they breed in the same culture. And one of

---

[5]Peter L. Berger, Brigitte Berger, and Hansfried Kellner, *The Homeless Mind: Modernization and Consciousness* (New York: Random House, 1973).

the alienations of which Berger et al. make much is that between public role and private person.[6]

The lack of unity we face lies not only between groups in our society but in the schizoid posture we come to take for granted in our own lives, so that in our carefully delineated roles, we are like the man possessed with a demon whose name was Legion (Mark 5:2–9). The gospel wills us not to live that kind of life. After Jesus casts out the demon, the gospel reports:

> They came to Jesus and saw the demoniac sitting there, clothed and in his right mind, the very man who had had the legion; and they were afraid. (Mark 5:15)

This is what Jesus does and what the church might be doing. He takes this man with a scattershot life and restores him to unity concerning his person. Notice the translation: "right mind." And notice also that when the others saw it, they were afraid. The world is afraid of right-minded—that is, single-minded—people. It depends on our schizoid mentality to keep things divided, with no single purpose for everyone. Berger et al. do not go so far in their analysis. But I believe it is implied in the statement that the world as we know it would collapse if we moved toward right-mindedness. The gospel is powerful, and we shall have to make up our minds. Perhaps we have too much invested in our fragmentation, but there is an alternative! And that's news. It's bad news because it means the dismantling of our world. It's good news because it invites us to new humanness.

Freedom *and* Unity

The promise of the gospel is that we may be both free and united. That is the substance of *shalom,* or at least that's the way we have stacked the cards here. That is an enormous promise, the one people in our time are waiting to hear. The promise of freedom is powerful to those who live coerced lives and are cut off from joy. The promise of unity is powerful to folks who are cut off from other people and from their own lives, who are frenzied and frantic because of their fragmentation. As one reflects on the promise of freedom and unity and on the problem of coercion and fragmentation, the intersection

---

[6]See the important distinction between "person" and "personage" made by Paul Tournier, *The Meaning of Persons* (New York: Harper, 1957).

of the two becomes clear. What I have learned from Berger et al.'s analysis is that coercion (the antithesis of freedom) and fragmentation (the antithesis of unity) belong together. It is when our lives are fragmented in the hopeless effort to serve too many gods and honor too many priorities that we are coerced. It is when we are driven to meet too many expectations and manipulated to meet too many standards that our lives become an endless chase with no important satisfactions anywhere. Jesus addressed the coercion in people's lives by freeing them of expectations that cheapened and eroded their humanity. He invited people to live uncoerced lives:

> "Do not worry about your life...But strive first for the kingdom of God and his righteousness, and all these things will be given to you as well." (Matthew 6:25a, 33)

> "You lack one thing; go, sell what you own, and give the money to the poor, and you will have treasure in heaven; then come, follow me." (Mark 10:21)

> "Come to me, all you that are weary and are carrying heavy burdens, and I will give you rest. Take my yoke upon you, and learn from me; for I am gentle and humble in heart, and you will find rest for your souls." (Matthew 11:28–29)

> Sin no more! (John 5:14, RSV)

Jesus presented to people the possibility of living free lives—not driven or frantic, but living responsibly where they found themselves.

But the end of coercion in their lives also required the end of fragmentation. And he announced that the end of fragmentation was possible as he called people away from idolatries, as his tradition had always done:

> "No one can serve two masters; for a slave will either hate the one and love the other, or be devoted to the one and despise the other. You cannot serve God and wealth." (Matthew 6:24)

> "And why do you break the commandment of God for the sake of your tradition?"(Matthew 15:3)

"Sell your possessions, and give alms. Make purses for yourselves that do not wear out, an unfailing treasure in heaven, where no thief comes near and no moth destroys. For where your treasure is, there your heart will be also." (Luke 12:33–34)

Shalom is the end of coercion. *Shalom* is the end of fragmentation. *Shalom* is the freedom to rejoice. *Shalom* is the courage to live an integrated life in a community of coherence. These are not simply neat values to be added on. They are a massive protest against the central values by which our world operates. The world depends on coercion. The world depends on fragmented loyalties. The world as presently ordered depends on those very conditions against which the gospel protests and to which it provides alternatives.

So we have this gospel of freedom and unity. It occurred to me that these two central dimensions of *shalom* pull in opposite directions. It is a promise of freedom, but freedom is surely "to do one's own thing." As we struggle for ourselves and for others, how do we permit persons to do their own thing without disrupting everything else? But unity is having it all together, all of us sharing in and celebrating what we have in common. The hard work of *shalom* is to keep these in balance and in tension with each other. Freedom without unity tends to be destructive self-seeking with no regard for others. Unity without freedom tends to be conformity that crushes the humanity and imagination of those involved. So the vision of humanness held here is authentic freedom, which is in the context of unity—powerful unity that takes seriously the freedom of persons. And we are still asking: Is such a community possible? Is it possible to be really free and really together all at the same time? In the meantime, we hassle one another for freedom, which becomes indifferent individualism, and for unity, which becomes oppressive conformity.

Freedom, of course, can be abusive, and as we prize freedom, we must be concerned for responsibility. The freedom to pollute must ask about clean air for others. The freedom to have a gun must ask about the safety of folks in the middle of the night. Freedom for sex must ask about dehumanization and respect for persons. So our freedom is always concerned with caring accountability. And unity must ask about justice, about the just due of each child of God, not only about folks staying in their place and keeping rules, but about having space in which to grow and dream and learn and work; not only about belonging, but belonging in ways that do not crush or manipulate. So Jesus does free and unite. But he frees people to responsibility. He unites people to perfect freedom.

It is clear in our family that some of us are tilted one way or another. Perhaps it is likely that younger people are tilted to freedom and older people are tilted to unity. Or is it that well-off people care for order and disadvantaged people cry out for liberty? In our family I am the unity guy: "Everybody eats at the same time. This is what a family does." And my wife is the freedom agent: "We will be more a family if people have latitude to come and go with a secure sense of belonging." So we struggle with our tilts, and we must keep them in tension.

Now having said all that, I have wondered if we have any models or experiences in which freedom and unity come together. I suggest that that is what the eucharist is about. The holy communion is our supreme experience of all of God's people coming together, not on our terms, but on God's terms. It is our vision of unity being actualized. But it is also the place of freedom, where every man, woman, and child comes face-to-face with the power of the risen Lord, celebrates baptism, and is set free to his or her own humanity. It is where we are intimately and powerfully together in freeing ways for the sake of the human spirit among us. So we say, "This is the joyful feast of the people of God. Come from the East and the West, and from the North and the South."[7] It is the joyful feast. We come in joy because here we are valued with our peculiar dignity and worth. But it is joy for a people with a common identity. And at the table, our joy and our commonness do not conflict. They are essential to each other. Thus, when we are at that table, we are fully in the presence of what *shalom* is like. And perhaps it is characteristic that such joy and commonality, such freedom and unity, must always happen "on the night when he was betrayed."[8]

At that table and in all our *shalom*, we focus finally on him who is the embodiment of *shalom*. He is not only the one who frees and

[7]Invitation from the Service of Word and Sacrament I of the United Church of Christ as found in *The Hymnal of the United Church of Christ* (Philadelphia: United Church Press, 1974), 20.

[8]Ibid., 21.

unites. He is the one who is free and united. He is free from all the claims and expectations of the world—the completely uncoerced person. He is also the united person, united in his person with a singleness of vision and commitment, united with his brothers and sisters in the pain and joy of the world—the completely unfragmented person. Not for nothing were all the people "spellbound by what they heard (Luke 19:48). The scandal of Jesus, and the offense of the gospel, was that he embodied (read "incarnated") the kind of personhood that the world not only does not have but must resist and actively oppose. Indeed, he embodies a notion of humanness that the world cannot tolerate, and therefore some people "kept looking for a way to kill him" (Luke 19:47). Most people took no offense at him, but those who had a vested interest in coercion and fragmentation did take offense at him (Luke 7:23). They could not tolerate the vision of wholeness, freedom, and reconciliation that he brought with him.

We must ask how it was that he had the power of freedom and the power of unity in his person. That could be articulated in many ways, but is the mystery of it not in his vulnerability? He sought nothing, asked nothing, feared nothing; he emptied himself and became obedient to death on a cross. And in his emptiness, his obedience, and his death, has come power toward life, toward freedom and unity. His vulnerability can hardly be tolerated by the world— not because he is unacceptable, but because he envisions the dismantling of the world, and that is too much. It is no wonder that we boldly resolve to change toward *shalom,* and at the same time we refuse with equal fervor to change at all. It has always been so with the vision. We have not yet decided whether or not we want to live uncoerced, unfragmented lives. We could!

4

ACTION IN THE BRICKYARD

Afterward Moses and Aaron went to Pharaoh and said, "Thus says the LORD, the God of Israel, 'Let my people go, so that they may celebrate a festival to me in the wilderness.'" But Pharaoh said, "Who is the LORD, that I should heed him and let Israel go? I do not know the LORD, and I will not let Israel go." Then they said, "The God of the Hebrews has revealed himself to us; let us go a three days' journey into the wilderness to sacrifice to the LORD our God, or he will fall upon us with pestilence or sword." But the king of Egypt said to them, "Moses and Aaron, why are you taking the people away from their work? Get to your labors!" Pharaoh continued, "Now they are more numerous than the people of the land and yet you want them to stop working!" That same day Pharaoh commanded the taskmasters of the people, as well as their supervisors, "You shall no longer give the people straw to make bricks, as before; let them go and gather straw for themselves. But you shall require of them the same quantity of bricks as they have made previously; do not diminish it, for they are lazy; that is why they cry, 'Let us go and offer sacrifice to our God.' Let heavier work be laid on them; then they will labor at it and pay no attention to deceptive words."

EXODUS 5:1–9

Now after John was arrested, Jesus came to Galilee, proclaiming the good news of God, and saying, "The time is fulfilled, and the kingdom of God has come near; repent, and believe in the good news."

MARK 1:14–15

One of the things a study of the Bible can do is to provide us with images that help us to understand better the flow and situation of our lives. *Shalom* is such an abstract word in our ears that we need to find ways to make it concrete. The Bible never talks about *shalom* in an abstract or fuzzy way. It is always very specific and concrete. Put negatively, that is the scandal of biblical faith, that if *shalom* is experienced, it is experienced very concretely. Put positively, this is what we mean in Christian faith when we talk about incarnation, that God's *shalom* is always embodied in such a way that people know it is happening in their historical experience.

The Drama of the Brickyard

The image I want to pursue with you now that may make *shalom* concrete as both scandal and incarnation is "brickyard." "Brickyard" is a remote image for those of us who mostly do not do physical labor, but we can still imagine it. I use the image to pursue the exodus event in the Old Testament; but before we talk about the exodus, let us try to get inside the tone and demand of the brickyard. A brickyard is a place of competent production. It is where bricks are made to specification and on schedule. If the workers there are treated well, they are supplied with the materials for their quota. If they are not treated well, they must even get their own materials (Exodus 5:7). That is what is meant by making "bricks without straw," not that they were inferior bricks but that in the same time frame as always, the Israelites had to both secure the material and to make the bricks. So the brickyard is a place of competent production where the production schedule is taken with great seriousness.

The brickyard is also a place of coercion and profit. It is profit for the people who own and sell the bricks and set the production schedule. But for the people who make the bricks, it is a place of coercion. That is, they are there to meet other people's standards, to knuckle under to others' demands. Here there is no zone of freedom, not even a hint of a break in the heat of the day. The gap between the people of profit and the people who are coerced is not an accident of the system, but is built into the design of the system. Most often the story of the brickyard is put out in company literature. Remarkably, the biblical story of the brickyard is told from the perspective of the coerced.

And because they are coerced, it follows that the brickyard is a place of unhappiness, oppression, and, of course, enormous hostility. Hostility inevitably comes with oppression and the weary, desperate recognition that I am not in charge of my own life, that I have no options, and that someone else is enjoying the immoral privilege of selecting my options for me. And at bottom, the brickyard is a place of hopelessness. Not only must we produce for the others, but there is no prospect, not in our wildest imagination, that things are ever going to change. There will never be enough bricks to meet the quota. There will never be enough profits to satisfy the regime. There will never be enough power to get rid of the pressure and demand. And so the alternatives in our lives are to make bricks and to suffer, or to refuse to make bricks and to suffer more. Sort of a Catch-22.

Not a single one of us is far removed from that set of realities. This image could be a powerful one for us precisely because it is like our own experience. We are each of us in the brickyard. We all owe our souls to the company store. It does not matter if it is a fifth grader with a demanding baseball coach or a third grader with a teacher who shouts or a father who demands; it does not matter if it is a taxpayer who is always playing catch-up or an unappreciated mother and wife. It does not matter if it is a graduate student never satisfying his or her committee, a junior executive under enormous pressure, a doctor with too many patients, a salesperson whose quota is always upped, or a social worker with a heavy workload. We are all of us caught in a way of life that yields only frantic hostility and desperate effort, which cannot finally pay off.

The symbol has power because we move in and out of brickyards. Sometimes we are the hopeless slave, never having a zone of freedom. Sometimes we are the owner, eyeing the quotas with eagerness, but always being inventive to find new ways of being anxious. It is a system that is obvious in public life, but which invades the dark recesses of our piety and our morality. Brickyards always seem to envelop us. And we go from one to another, but the space between is narrow and soon gone.

Everybody thought it had to be like that. The slaves and the owners. It had always been so and still is today, isn't it? But the Bible, the announcement of *shalom,* raises an unheard-of question. You can see the small crowd gathering in the yard, and even the foreman comes over, partly in fear, partly in curiosity. And there is that stranger with a strange question. It could have been Moses or anybody with any name, because what counted is what he said: "Let my people go!" That is what he said. And the moment it was said, the brickyard was changed. And it will never be the same again. That is the good news, good news for the slaves, but also for the foreman. The brickyard has been completely transformed by that announcement: "Let my people go!" That is the beginning of *shalom:* a brickyard in which that statement is uttered.

The word traveled quickly to the big house. Pharaoh himself came to see the brickyard, and he noticed immediately that things were changed. So he joined the issue immediately. It seemed to be Moses versus the foreman. But it was quickly escalated to Pharaoh versus Moses, and then it became clear that it was Yahweh, the God of Freedom, versus the gods of Egypt. And each had a program for the brickyard. It was "Let my people go" versus "Make more bricks." It mattered (and still matters decisively) who won that contest, because the outcome would determine forever the character and quality of life in the brickyard.

The drama of the brickyard revolves around the question, *Who is in charge?* If the Egyptian gods, the gods of coercion and oppression, are in charge, then there is nothing to do but to make bricks. But if Yahweh is in charge, then it is time to sing and dance and be free. So the issue is joined:

> [Moses turned the water to blood.] But the magicians of Egypt did the same by their secret arts; so Pharaoh's heart remained hardened, and he would not listen to them. (Exodus 7:22)

The suspense mounts, but the action is duplicated:

> [Moses and Aaron brought frogs on the land.] But the magicians did the same by their secret arts, and brought frogs up on the land of Egypt. (Exodus 8:7)

So far it was a standoff, point for point, but it was only warm-up time. Then they moved to the next event:

[Moses and Aaron brought gnats on the land.] The magicians tried to produce gnats by their secret arts, but *they could not.* (Exodus 8:18)

They could not! Imagine that! The ones who had always owned the brickyards were shown not to have the real power. The word spread all over the brickyard, and it was a decisive moment in the history of the brickyard. The powers of coercion were defeated. The power of Yahweh was superior. He was in charge! *Shalom* had come to the brickyard, and things were topsy-turvy. The old quota system was gone. Coercive, fearful power was overthrown. The end of oppression and hostility. But most of all the end of despair and the birth of hope. If this could happen in our brickyard, where it seemed that nothing good could happen, then anything leading toward freedom can happen anywhere under any circumstances. And note—note above all—this is not a change of attitude, nor simply of perception. This is a real change of power, a decisive redistribution of power, an abrupt disruption of political and economic arrangements. Brickyards are no longer for coercion, but for freedom. And then the slaves left and hurried out to the wilderness on the way to the mountain of obligation and the land of promise. They made it to the first place, to new obligations, quickly. The promise was a long way off, but the brickyard was transformed.

In our tradition we cannot talk about *shalom* without talking about exodus; and when we talk about exodus, we affirm that the brickyard has become the place where the question of power is asked: "Who is in charge here?" And the question is answered: "My name is 'Let-my-people-go!'" And "Let-my-people-go" is now in charge.

Our forebears—our mothers and fathers—have spent the centuries since that event pondering what it means. That is really the task of theology—to face the issue. What does it mean that the Lord of Freedom controls the brickyards? Of course it says something about this Lord. It says that "Let-my-people-go" is powerful and for us. It says to us: "Get out from under the load of oppression and coercion." This Lord's intention is that we should not have to lead that kind of life, no matter how much the technological, bureaucratic propaganda of the regime lays on us. This Lord is for freedom and is powerful enough to introduce freedom into the grimmest brickyard there could be. That is the odd faith of the children of Israel to which we are heirs. It says that the Lord has not abandoned the world and placed the power of life and the mystery of being at the disposal of the oppressive agents in the world.

But what that says about us! It affirms to us that we can never secure our existence nor order our brickyard by more quotas. We can't do it in the brickyards over which we preside. Nor can we do it in the brickyards where we are on the other end of things. We can't secure our own existence by our productivity and our hustle, nor by our loyalty to the owners of the yard. The capacity to secure our existence has not been turned over to us. The Lord has retained that. That, of course, is what we do not like. How convenient if it had been turned over to us. What has apparently been turned over to us is the capacity to destroy ourselves. But the Lord has not placed in our hands the comparable power to make our lives safe, whole, free. This is kept by God, who gives it in strange times and places. The supreme fact about us, which the slaves discovered that night in Egypt, is that our well-being, our salvation, our *shalom,* is hidden in God's holy mystery, which none of our best efforts can penetrate or explain.

We know this name—Yahweh—which is shorthand for "Let my people go." But we know this name only because Yahweh told us. And when we were told, it was enigmatic, so that we knew nothing about the source or character of this incredible power. We know a name and we guess at its meaning. The most we know is that Let-my-people-go comes to the brickyards and calls us to shift the basis of our being in the world. The victory won over the forces of Egypt is strange and never seems quite clear. But on the basis of that unclear victory by that one with the enigmatic name, we are called to forge a new life, choose a new identity, walk a new path on the way to the desert where Yahweh will meet us with a strange, ten-sided notion of freedom.

So who is really in charge? Answer carefully, because we are expected to give an extraordinary answer. But if that answer is the right one, then every other answer is wrong. To suggest that any other is in charge, to name any other name other than the Lord of disrupting, abiding freedom, is to answer wrongly. It is to embrace *idolatry.* Idolatry is at the heart of oppression and coercion. Idolatry is at the root of both our oppressing and our being oppressed. Idolatry—wrongly perceiving who is in charge—is the opposite of *shalom. Shalom,* as we are invited to perceive it, is premised on knowing who is in charge and making the life-reorienting pilgrimage to the mountain of freedom and obligation.

Talk about brickyards and idolatry, about deserts and mountains, about freedom and obligation—that is not the usual rhetoric of the Christian community. I want simply to affirm that while the vocabulary may sound a bit different, the issues are the same in the New Testament articulation of our faith. Only we have so beclouded the issue of power in the Christian gospel that we have been blinded to the question of the gospel: "Who is in charge here?" So let me comment on how that same issue dominates the gospel memories in the New Testament.

The Gospel and the Brickyard

Let us talk about the frame of the gospel of Mark. It begins, as scholars have agreed, with this incredible statement:

The time is fulfilled, and the kingdom of God has come near; repent, and believe in the good news. (Mark 1:15)

Hear that statement as though it were announced in the brickyard. It is the time for management change. Jesus comes to the brickyard and posts the sign: "Under new management." Or more dramatically, it is as though he came to end colonialism, to take down the old flag of the empire and send the governor packing. The time is at hand to face the radical reorientation of it all. It is kingdom time. It is time for God's kingdom, the same God who did in Pharaoh, the same God still at work on behalf of freedom and against every form of coercion. The gospel begins with the same announcement. It is time to face the fact that a new policy is being implemented, a policy that ends all coercion.

The battle raged, and it was by no means clear how it would turn out. Decisively on the cross, the gospel of Mark presents the coercive, chaotic powers having their day. And, indeed, it seemed on Friday night that they had won, that the voice of freedom was silenced in the land. But the gospel has the right word at the right place. Jesus, dead on the cross, clearly defeated, was abandoned by all, by all except one Roman soldier, a man under authority, who was used to determining who was in charge. From his mouth comes this incredible conclusion: "Truly this man was God's Son!" (Mark 15:39). Now finally, in a moment of death and abandonment, the crucial issue was settled. Now it was clear that the God of Freedom was in charge, and the powers of coercion, though strong, could not prevail.

What did the soldier see there that day in Jerusalem? What one always sees in a brickyard. The voices of coercion and competence and production always are the loud ones. But he was callous to those noises and unimpressed. He cut through them to see that even in this ruthless brickyard, the power of freedom won out. Because what happened to him that day did not occur in a vacuum. It had continuity with all else he had done. And he knew what the facts seemed to deny—that the answer to the question of power was settled already on Friday, settled in his favor.

These two texts comprise Jesus' inaugural and his valedictory:

- Repent, the kingdom has come near.
- Truly this was God's Son.

They are the same kind of statements. Both affirm who is in charge. Both are unlikely and unconvincing, either in the mouth of a lonely soldier or in the mouth of an itinerant preacher. But consider what holds them together! Between Mark 1:14–15 and 15:39 is a long series of encounters with the sick, the possessed, the lepers, the dead, the guilty, the ungrateful. The two statements are held together by Jesus' contact with incompetents. That is what all those people have in common. They are incompetent. And you know about incompetents in the brickyard. They can't make bricks, so they are not valued. But the radicalness of Jesus' message is in this. Not just in freedom, but in valuing the incompetents. He enjoyed being with them. He took them seriously. He valued them.

And in valuing them he called into question all the other values. There are certain correlates we may observe about the way the world is organized. Coercion depends on competence. Coercion and competence meet in their valuing of both quality and quantity. That is what holds it all together: coercion, competence, quality, quantity, quota. And Jesus, like Yahweh back in Egypt, rejected the whole business. No more coercion. He freed folks from that. No more competence. He obviously wasn't interested in that. No more interest in quotas. The rejection of the very values that have given us the good life. The rejection of things that make us successful, comfortable, affluent, respectable. That is the nature of the new management, kingdom management:

- People are not valued for their competence.
- Nobody is impressed with quotas.
- Nobody is worried about not meeting the quotas.

Finally, all exodus talk has to bring us face-to-face with the resurrection. The resurrection is the ultimate resolution of the question of who's in charge. The surprise of the resurrection is that the people who seemed to be in charge on "Good" Friday turned out not to be in charge. Maybe this is what the centurion was discerning sooner than the rest. Maybe he discerned what the world normally misses— that the apparent victory of Friday couldn't last.

The version of the event in Matthew provides a remarkable detail. What the centurion observed, according to Matthew, was this:

> The tombs also were opened, and many bodies of the saints who had fallen asleep were raised. After his resurrection they came out of the tombs and entered the holy city and appeared to many. (Matthew 27:52–53)

Think of that—the victory did not wait until Sunday, because already on Friday the dead came out of the tombs! That is how it was in Egypt. That is how it was every time Jesus came to an incompetent and restored him or her to full value and full citizenship. The dead are surely the people whom the world has dismissed as irrelevant. Recall, for example, *The Invisible Man,* the one whom people do not see because they have written him off as worthless.[1] The crucifixion-resurrection was an event of release and valuing for all those whom the world had declared incompetent, worthless, and therefore invisible. The centurion knew that anybody who can bring the dead to life, who can value the incompetents who can't make it in the system, anybody who can do that has been entrusted with the power and mystery of God.

Matthew has one other observation about resurrection. If resurrection is the final settlement of the power issue, it should not

---

[1]Ralph Ellison, *The Invisible Man* (New York: Random House, 1947). It is the story of how society can ignore and will to nonbeing or death "undesirable" or unvalued members. Such a destruction involves no physical harm, but massive disregard and excommunication.

surprise us. He observes that resurrection is bad news for governors. In fact, they can't tolerate resurrections!

"If this comes to the governor's ears, we will satisfy him and keep you out of trouble." (Matthew 28:14)

Resurrections are great for dead and incompetent and devalued people, but not for governors and other people who run brickyards, intent to have a resurrectionless arena in which the way of the world still counts and there are quotas and coercion and all the rest. But resurrection is what it's about:

- Resurrection is the end of quotas.
- Resurrection can get people in trouble.
- Resurrection is valuing nobodies.
- Resurrection is the realm of radical newness and the abrupt end of oldness.
- Resurrection is a statement about who is in charge.

That is the proclamation that could change the world, and it is what *shalom* is about. It is the substance of our faith and the drive of our ministry. When we say *shalom,* we utter words the governor does not want to hear. But let me be clear. This kind of resolution of power and this kind of freedom are not about careless talk of dismantling institutions. Nor are they about the mindless kind of self-indulgence that poses as freedom for those who don't give a damn. Rather, they are about the kind of freedom that calls us to risk, to stand and gather around the new option in the brickyards where the issue is not yet decided. Mostly we live in brickyards where the magicians can do as well as the ones sent by Yahweh. And besides, we are not always the coerced slave. Sometimes we are the governor with a clipboard.

No wonder the resolution of the power question toward freedom troubles us. It is bad news and fills us with rage, all of us. But it is also good news. And it leads us to doxology. All of us.

5

Our Story Tells Us What to Do

The Egyptians urged the people to hasten their departure from the land, for they said, "We shall all be dead." So the people took their dough before it was leavened, with their kneading bowls wrapped up in their cloaks on their shoulders. The Israelites had done as Moses told them; they had asked the Egyptians for jewelry of silver and gold, and for clothing, and the LORD had given the people favor in the sight of the Egyptians, so that they let them have what they asked. And so they plundered the Egyptians.

The Israelites journeyed from Rameses to Succoth, about six hundred thousand men on foot, besides children. A mixed crowd also went up with them, and livestock in great numbers, both flocks and herds. They baked unleavened cakes of the dough that they had brought out of Egypt; it was not leavened, because they were driven out of Egypt and could not wait, nor had they prepared any provisions for themselves.

The time that the Israelites had lived in Egypt was four hundred thirty years. At the end of four hundred thirty years, on that very day, all the companies of the LORD went out from the land of Egypt.

That was for the LORD a night of vigil, to bring them out of the land of Egypt. That same night is a vigil to be kept for the LORD by all the Israelites throughout their generations.

EXODUS 12:33–42

The questions of what we ought to do and how to decide it have always been difficult. For biblical faith, the "ought" of life received its basic form one lost night in ancient Egypt when a slave mother came into the hovel where her children were sleeping, covered their mouths to keep them quiet, awakened them, and said, "Come, we're going now."

It was a dark and awesome night, filled with risk and fear. It began with a quiet gathering of all the slave families and then a panicky rush to the border with the Egyptian guards in hot pursuit. When the slaves reached the other side, they were free! Most thought they would never make it. And they got out their tambourines and danced. They sang and they prayed. They gave thanks to God (Exodus 15:1; Psalm 105:43).

All the rest of biblical history is telling again the incredible story of that night of fear and freedom and the morning of joy and dancing. Sometimes it is the patient retelling of the story so that the young can own it as their story. As in Deuteronomy 26:5–9, the story of the exodus always passes easily from "them" to "us" in the telling; it is always our story and never "their" story. It is about us, and we remember being awakened in the night. Sometimes it involves the urgent probing of adults asking what the story means in a quite different situation where the implications are not at all clear (Amos 2:6–16; Hosea 11:1–9; Micah 6:1–8). And it takes remarkable imagination to make the connections, because the story never gives clear rules or guidance. It insists only that we remember who we have been and who we have become; that is the way of morality in the Bible. Sometimes it is the passionate doxology of freedom. Sometimes it is the pitiful groan of knowing that exoduses don't happen much anymore.

In any case, those of the biblical faith know that the basic "ought" of life emerges where one is met by the Holy One. They know also that the Holy One meets us most surely, most powerfully, most unmistakably in exodus kinds of events. It is here that our slaveries are turned to freedom, that our desperate lostness is displaced by the delight of being found, that our sense of death is overwhelmed by the dance of life. And it often happens in the night of our lives when we sleep the sleep of slavery and dream the dream of freedom, and we awaken out of the nightmare.

Those same families (when they finished their doxology at the water) continued to the desolation of Sinai, where the Holy One of freedom met them again. You know that meeting where the ten commands of biblical faith emerged. But what we don't observe carefully enough is that the context of the "oughts" is "I am the LORD your God, who brought you out of the land of Egypt" (Exodus 20:2; Deuteronomy 5:6). Biblical morality is not found in the Ten Commandments or in any part of them, but in the action of the Holy One. Sinai is a probing of what the exodus means. In my judgment, this is the key to understanding morality in a biblical context. Sinai is specific and demanding, but its claim and its power are of the exodus variety.

When we speak of the collapse of morality, we are probably talking about the deadness and failure of the "oughts" when they have been torn apart from the power of the Holy One. The "oughts" of Sinai have no claim on those who do not remember being awakened in the night of fear and the ensuing freedom to dance in the morning on the other side of the water. When the freedom story is about someone else, it makes no claim on us.

Or, to change the image, biblical morality is in a story rather than a set of rules. It is like that in our families as well. How we act is generally not determined by what our parents told us to do, but by the events that shaped our growing up in the family. In the Bible it is a story cherished and remembered, a story about our faith family, little faith-cousins awakened in the night, faith-uncles and faith-aunts who crossed the water and danced in incredulity. Morality is based on the assurance that that story is our story, not simply remembered, but a story we experience—being awakened in the night, called to dangerous waters, and then to dance again.

Of course, it takes eyes to see. Exoduses are happening all around us—of a personal kind, in the pain and delight of growing up; of a social kind, in the upheavals and changes that make persons free and open up institutions; of a visible, external kind; and of a hidden, internal kind. The Holy One, within and without, has not stopped freeing people and calling them to rejoice.

Perhaps those are the images an Old Testament teacher would use. Then change the picture only slightly and put it this way: Biblical morality begins with a child rushing into the kitchen. He has just been down the street, and he must tell his mother breathlessly what he saw. The old beggar, a fixture for decades at the city well, was just touched by a rabbi, and he was healed (John 5:1–9). The child rushes home and, in a glow, with the words tumbling out, concludes: "Imagine, healing right in our town!" The whole family comes to hear, and no doubt they dance too, because we don't expect real healing to come that close to us.

Or is it a strange cluster of people in the street? They are arguing; some are scared. But the main character answers so simply and so finally, "One thing I do know, that though I was blind, now I see" (John 9:25). And they dance the exodus dance!

One more scenario. A woman comes rushing home shocked and confused and a little hysterical. She is speechless. Finally they get the story from her. The tomb is empty! Jesus is alive (Matthew 28:1–10). Here begins morality. Our "ought" is not derived from a bunch of rules. But when incredible healing comes so close to us, we accept a new claim made on us.

All these scenes have a common element. They tell of an unexplainable turn in people's lives—a turn toward wholeness, a turn unexpected and sometimes unwanted, a turn nobody could have imagined or made for oneself. Some would say "miracle"; some would call it "salvation."

They are the rare moments when life is turned toward wholeness. They are precious moments made for sharing and for dancing, for telling and retelling, for giving to others. They are all over the Bible, and they are the root of our "ought." Our "ought" moves from the gift of *shalom,* which comes to us in incredible ways. We can miss it very easily.

I found it strange, in writing this, that it was natural to speak about the excitement of children and the surprise of women. I wonder if the notion of masculinity in our culture—the need to master, control, and hustle—is antiexodus and antiresurrection, and so antimorality. When we are uptight about schedules and appointments, exoduses are hard to come by. We are too busy, too cynical, too committed to making it in our slavery to dream the dream of freedom; and we never notice how much slavery is a nightmare that does not have to be. The exodus symbol, or the symbol of resurrection, is not just an opening to new ways of being. It is also a judgment on the old ways of being, which makes us so anxious and fearful that we can never risk leaving in the night.

Such events, exodus or resurrection, are glimpses of the Holy One, whom we come to know in the turning of our lives toward wholeness. Such a notion of the Holy One is a distinctive, if not peculiar, notion of who God is. It means that we do not perceive God as a rule-giver, as an establisher of right and wrong, or as guarantor of the status quo. Rather, God acts in the moment of the turn. And the rest of our faith consists of reflection on those moments in which our lives are changed. Such moments address us and insist that we be transformed. Such events claim us. They overwhelm us with a demand, which then comes to be morality:

- Free people can't live like slave people.
- A man who can see can't act like a blind man.
- A live person can't settle for a morality of death.
- A son found again can't play the part of a lost one.

A people claimed, loved, and identified can't live like nonentities. So morality is sorting out the demands and claims that emerge out of the precious moments when life is whole and new. Consider how we would act if we were to live according to our exodus. Sinai provides some clues:

- Exodus people honor the Sabbath, because it is a reminder of the contrast between oppressive work and healing, humane rest.
- Exodus people don't covet, because the tyranny of Pharaoh was in coveting after he had had enough.
- Exodus people don't steal, kill, or commit adultery, because now they know that life is too precious to be abused and perverted.

The laws of Israel are informed by exodus:

"You shall not oppress a resident alien…for you were aliens in the land of Egypt." (Exodus 23:9)

"You shall also love the stranger, for you were strangers in the land of Egypt." (Deuteronomy 10:19)

Much of Israel's morality is concerned with the disinherited in society—widows, orphans, sojourners, all outsiders—and the clue to treating them is Israel's own experience of being an outsider. Much of Israel's morality is concerned with self-serving pride, and the clue to understanding pride is that it will lead to the tyranny they knew under Pharaoh.

Among the laws and moral teachings, exodus is occasionally mentioned. Even when it isn't explicit, it is always hovering in our awareness as we are reminded of the dangers of exploitation (Amos 2:6–8), of coveting (Isaiah 5:8–9), of fickleness (Hosea 7:11). Life is lived by the model and the power of the exodus. When that model no longer controls, it means that the story has lost its power. We have forgotten who we are. The story now appears to be about someone else; we no longer celebrate the story as being about us.

It is no different in the early church of the New Testament. It is the power of the resurrection that calls us to cope with evil creatively (Romans 12:9–21). It is the power of the resurrection that lets people heal other people, as when Peter says that remarkable word "walk" (Acts 3:6). It is the turn of new life that enables us to live lives characterized by joy, peace, patience, self-control (Galatians 5:22–23). The entire morality of the New Testament is rooted in freedom, the freedom of the exodus and the freedom of the resurrection. "For freedom Christ has set us free. Stand firm, therefore, and do not submit again to a yoke of slavery" (Galatians 5:1).

The memories preserved for us of Jesus' own ministry are a staggering sequence of exodus and resurrection events. He casts out demons and so calls a man back to a life of humanness (Mark 5:1–13). He heals lepers, which means he breaks the social barriers that exclude the "unclean" (Mark 1:40–41). He frees his friends from the terror of fear by an act of power over a storm (Mark 4:35–41). All of which is summarized in a remarkable way: "…the blind receive their sight, the lame walk, the lepers are cleansed, the deaf hear, the dead are raised, the poor have good news brought to them" (Luke 7:22).

That's morality, but of a very strange kind. Nothing about keeping rules or being good. Everything about delivering persons to freedom. Everything raising persons to new life. Jesus calls his followers to a like kind of morality, which delivers from demons, and which heals (Mark 6:13). This morality grows out of the conviction that the world need not be the way it is. It is a morality charged with transforming the world, with overcoming the powers of slavery and evil that box us in and prevent us from being human. Being moral means to be engaged seriously in the transformation of the world for the sake of humanness. The New Testament calls that "life in the kingdom." It is a call to an unheard-of kind of life that questions our old commitments and invites us to more freedom than most of us are ready to embrace.

But this freedom is not license, or irresponsibility, or copping out, or doing our own thing. "'All things are lawful,' but not all things are beneficial" (1 Corinthians 10:23, au. trans.). This is the test and measure of our freedom, that it is one of helping, of edifying, of letting humanness emerge. Moral acts are those that cause new exoduses and new resurrections. Immorality consists in actions that are antiexodus and antiresurrection—that do not free or that free in destructive ways.

The tricky demand in all this is that the Bible never settles for a morality that deals simply with individuals. It always asks about social structures, about government and law and social policy, about institutions that can cause exoduses or prevent them. Today that is the part of morality that tears at the church. We are often eager to confine the claim of biblical morality to private questions of right and wrong. We have a *long* history of thinking that we can privatize morality and settle for personal virtues of purity and honesty. But the deep issues of biblical morality consistently concern the public, social dimensions of exodus. Pharaoh's problem is not personal impurity, but a state system of institutional tyranny. The prophets condemn Israel for perverted courts (Micah 3:11) and inequitable real estate practices (Micah 2:1–4; 1 Kings 21). Jesus' quarrel with the establishment of his time, which finally killed him, was that it had substituted private virtue for social concern, and such perverted morality prevents resurrection (Matthew 23:13–28).

The catch, of course, is that private morality as it is usually defined fits nicely with our vested interests. By contrast, questions of institutional morality often collide with our investments. But it can't be any other way. Resurrection and exodus are public events that call into question the structure and ordering of society. Thus, they address us at the places in our lives that demand most, and where we frequently resist most.

The moral issues of our time are difficult and will continue to be so. They are difficult because they are complex and we don't have all the data. They are also difficult because they call into question our little systems, and that scares us. It scares us because exoduses are all around us—of the young, African American, poor, female, the emotionally disturbed—the many people wanting to be free as God wills them to be. And as we ponder the threat of those forms of freedom, we discover that none of the rest of us is free either.

The Bible contains no solutions to such problems, but it gives us an angle of vision. Such moral questions will continue to be difficult and scary for all of us. But people who make bricks all the time for Pharaoh find the questions more difficult and more scary than people who dance the dance of freedom. Sometimes we are so busy making bricks that we don't even hear the music. It makes me wonder how many exoduses I have missed out on as I looked with wonderment at my bricks.

Morality is difficult because all the old guidebooks seem to have collapsed, or at least they seem inadequate. The frontier practice of defense by gun doesn't apply in an urban society. Old practices of having all the things you can have won't work in an overcrowded world. Old notions of a just war and "victory" are patently obsolete in a world of cruise missiles and smart bombs. And "all of them under their vines and fig trees" (1 Kings 4:25) is a vision that should be modified in the midst of a pollution that is not good for growing things. Nobody has the authority to announce morality any more. Our church has rightly discerned in this a faith crisis.

Persons and congregations in faith crisis are ready to face the old stories again in their power and let them make their claim. One never knows when one will be awakened in the night with the whisper, "Come, we're going now." Or when some child will burst into the room saying, "Healing has come to our town!" And then we shall dance the dance of freedom. And we shall know the Lord of the Commandments as the Lord of the Dance, the one who frees and calls us to remarkable "oughts."

PART THREE

A Vision of Order

6

ORDERING AND EATING

When Joseph came home, they brought him the present that they had carried into the house, and bowed to the ground before him. He inquired about their welfare, and said, "Is your father well, the old man of whom you spoke? Is he still alive?" They said, "Your servant our father is well; he is still alive." And they bowed their heads and did obeisance. Then he looked up and saw his brother Benjamin, his mother's son, and said, "Is this your youngest brother, of whom you spoke to me? God be gracious to you, my son!" With that, Joseph hurried out, because he was overcome with affection for his brother, and he was about to weep. So he went into a private room and wept there. Then he washed his face and came out; and controlling himself he said, "Serve the meal." They served him by himself, and them by themselves, and the Egyptians who ate with him by themselves, because the Egyptians could not eat with the Hebrews, for that is an abomination to the Egyptians. When they were seated before him, the firstborn according to his birthright and the youngest according to his youth, the men looked at one another in amazement. Portions were taken to them from Joseph's table, but Benjamin's portion was five times as much as any of theirs. So they drank and were merry with him.

GENESIS 43:26–34

He said also to the one who had invited him, "When you give a luncheon or a dinner, do not invite your friends or your brothers or your relatives or rich neighbors, in case they may invite you in return, and you would be repaid. But when you give a banquet, invite the poor, the crippled, the lame, and the blind. And you will be blessed, because they cannot repay you, for you will be repaid at the resurrection of the righteous."

LUKE 14:12–14

The *shalom* emphasis is an occasion in the church to think differently about our lives. One fresh way of doing that involves the theme of chaos and order, a theme very big in the Bible. The people in the Bible had, like us, a fear of chaos and a craving for order. And sometimes we prefer any order to any appearance of chaos.

If we are to be seriously engaged with our faith, we must be more sensitized to central *shalom* questions: How are things ordered? How did they get that way? Who wants to keep it that way? For what vested reason do they want to keep it that way? *Shalom* leads us to raise issues of sociology of value and sociology of power. I believe we have a chance in the life of the church to sensitize people to these matters, to help them recognize that things are not eternally ordered to be the way they are now. Rather, things are the way they are now because someone made them so, and we may assume they did so for some reason, good or ill. If I understand the current discussions of the theology of hope, they are centered in the conviction that things do not need to remain as they are and that if things have been made the way they are, they may be unmade from that form and ordered in another way. A theology of despair, to take the antithesis, is the dreadful conclusion that things are hopeless, that they are given and must be ordered as they are now. Such a conclusion is to abandon any hope for newness and to decide that the world is closed off from newness. *Shalom* is rooted in a theology of hope, in the powerful, buoyant conviction that the world can and will be transformed and renewed, that life can and will be changed, and newness can and will come.

How are things ordered now? All around us things are ordered, and mostly we accept that order in unthinking obedience. On the door of my favorite drive-in restaurant is a sign: "No Shoes, No Shirt— No Service—No Exceptions!" That is a statement of how things are ordered. Although that is relatively innocuous, I can remember, as many still can, a more diabolic statement of order: "We reserve the right to refuse service to anyone," or more blatantly, "Whites only." In retrospect those signs about ordering our chaos around "to refuse service" are ludicrous. How did we tolerate that? We didn't just tolerate it. We accepted it as an eternal given, not because we approved, but because we like order and are not accustomed to questioning it. We are not sensitized to the sociological dimensions of order and value.

I have wondered if some day soon, the current sign, "No Shoes, No Shirt..." will appear equally ludicrous. Be that as it may, I have wondered about that sign. Somebody powerful enough to make order has posted that sign, and surely for a reason. And I'm middle-class enough and middle-aged enough to approve their reasoning. *I* don't want to eat my hamburger looking at the unpleasantness of "dirty, barefoot, long-haired kids." Nonetheless, it is an imposed order and it is for a reason.

The issues have changed very sharply in the church. Recently it was all "out there" in the world. But now it is "in here," and every society and group directing the church must answer the question, Who can come "in here"? Because "in here" is where the goodies are. My favorite restaurant has decided who will have access to the goodies. Here is the point: The church must consist of people sensitized to the real rules of who has access to the goodies and who makes the rules about who has access. It is a decision made in every group, every family, every church. Somebody decides who has access to the goodies, and it is also decided who makes those decisions. And if *shalom* is about changing things, as it surely is, clearly we have a task of perception before we can begin the task of transformation. We must see clearly how somebody has taken a situation and has ordered it in a certain way. At least theoretically it could have been ordered in a variety of other ways.

It is not accidental that the sign I first noticed was on the door of a restaurant. Perhaps in eating more than in anything else, we act out our sense of order and our valuing of goodies and access to goodies. In eating, we engage in the most primal event of being insiders, and without knowing it we order our eating most carefully, as has my drive-in. It is in the elemental act of eating that we make our fundamental decisions about what we mean by *shalom*.

1. Covenant making in the Old Testament is characteristically done by covenant meal. "Those whom the gods would value, they first eat with." Thus, Exodus 24:11: On Mt. Horeb, "They beheld God, and they ate and drank."[1]
2. The early church knew Jesus best in the "breaking of bread" (Luke 24:28–35). And since that time this meal has been the most fundamental thing Christians do. It is around that table that we have had our greatest conflicts because we know intuitively that in eating and drinking we are choosing our brand of *shalom* and legitimating an ordering of our world.
3. In the 1960s in America, out of all the hassles and resistances about integration, it was that of "lunch counters" that became the symbolic issue. We knew intuitively that with whom we eat is a highly symbolic act expressing the covenants we honor and the shape of *shalom* we affirm and choose. As you know, for a time we settled for "vertical integration." We would stand together to eat, but not sit. I assume that was what our Puritan forebears called a "half-way covenant."

Eating is at the center of human life. There we do our choosing and our shaping of life. Older traditions such as the *Evangelical and Reformed Book of Worship* made the powerful statement that eucharist deals not merely with signs but with the reality that such worshipful signs represent. In that older, more tranquil language, we affirmed at the table that we were engaged in our primal ordering event. All through our eating we know that we have to do with the innermost sanctuary of our experience. On purely phenomenological grounds, apart from theology, we talk about "Real Presence" at the table. At the table is where the Lord really is. Think what it means when that awareness is coupled with this sign at our table: "No Shoes, No Shirt— No Service—No Exceptions." *Shalom* concerns ordering arrangements that control access to the goodies.

In that context, the Bible often presents eating as a *shalom* event.

In the Joseph narrative in Genesis, Joseph is eager to see his brothers, and when they meet, they have important exchanges. He is not yet identified as their brother, but he knows them. Then, as the

---

[1] I am not persuaded by Ernest Nicholson's argument in "The Interpretation of Exodus XXIV 9–11," *Vetus Testamentum* 24 (1974): 77–97, that Exodus 24:11 is not concerned with covenant making. While he argues cogently, the balance of evidence seems to me to be against his contention.

great prime minister, he says, "Serve the meal." In anticipation, one would guess he would be known to them in the breaking of bread. But the text has this:

> They served him by himself, and them by themselves, and the Egyptians who ate with him by themselves, because the Egyptians could not eat with the Hebrews, for that is an abomination to the Egyptians...Portions were taken to them from Joseph's table. (Genesis 43:32, 34)

Here is the first run of the movie *Separate Tables,* or should we say simply an early case of "separate but equal"? The little town where I grew up had one establishment, a tavern-coffee shop-pool hall, where the real decisions were made. In frequent if not constant session, were the key people from the American Legion, the church council, the civic club, and the school board. They were the only groups represented because there were no other formal groups. And mostly it was the same people in all these groups. In the back was an annex for Negroes (that is what we called them), served from the same kitchen by the same management. But that was a room of plain pipe racks, one lone light bulb, no jukebox, and only the groans of weary drunks or the loud laughter of people trying to enjoy themselves (or was it simply escape for a night?). And the food was brought to them from the same kitchen. "Portions were taken to them from Joseph's table," but never was there entry to the real goodies, no approach to the decision-making tables in the white section. There was real power, and it was the primal act of ordering the community, and nobody in either section of the tavern missed the message. Everybody understood about eating and shaping life and about who ordered community life and who did not.

Genesis 46:34 has evidence of the same kind of discrimination. The precise meaning of the text is uncertain because it asserts that shepherds were an abomination and keepers of cattle were not. There is some evidence to the contrary, but if we take simply that clause as it stands, it relates to our theme: "All shepherds are abhorrent to the Egyptians." We have glorified the shepherds in our Christmas pageants. But in fact, they are the outcasts—uneducated, dirty, repulsive, even intimidating. They are excluded from everything, including eating, because they have no marketable skills, nothing society values. And so when we plan and order our cities, in Egypt or elsewhere, we will order them so that the shepherds are in Goshen, and we do not need to see them again.

It doesn't take much imagination to see in this the kind of segregation and discrimination so pervasive in our situation. But my theme is not race. It is rather that in our primal activities, such as eating, we eat and drink and create the order we call *shalom,* carefully circumscribed by our values, fears, and wants. And when we do that, some are in, and some are out. Some have access to the goodies, and some are excluded from the goodies. And the big word is *abhorrent;* we exclude that which repels us, which makes us turn away in shame or fear or embarrassment. And every idea of *shalom* we conjure has made decisions about our repulsions and abominations. So it is good for us to check to see what we have excluded by what we have embraced. As usual, the abomination that moves us to action is not what is an abomination to Yahweh, but rather an abomination to the court, to the Egyptians, to the ones with power. And as we fashion life—that part over which we have power—we make arrangements to remove repulsion. First, we require it by law and then we legitimate it by religion. We transcend sociology of value and call it a given. First it is an abomination to the Egyptians, and then we call it an abomination to God. It is such an easy step to take from a table ordered by "No shoes, no shirt—no service—no exceptions," to a religious taboo.

The Joseph narrative in this regard is curious, all about the excluded Hebrews and the powerful, impressive Egyptians who posted the sign of exclusion. There was grist there for a good bit of reflection, such as, What does it mean to be a Hebrew and not an Egyptian? The narrative makes several affirmations that I want to note, for the Bible dares to suggest that the outsiders have the action: "The LORD blessed the Egyptian's house for Joseph's sake" (Genesis 39:5).[2] Joseph is still an outsider, but he becomes the reason for well-being on the inside.

"But the more they were oppressed, the more they multiplied and spread, so that the Egyptians came to dread the Israelites" (Exodus 1:12). There is movement here. Earlier they simply were repelled by the idea of Hebrews and didn't want to see them. And now they are scared. They won't look at them. They refuse to acknowledge their presence or even their existence. It is like the United States' refusing

---

[2]Hans Walter Wolff, in "The Kerygma of the Yahwist," *Interpretation* 20 (1966) has pursued the blessing motif in this and a number of other J texts in Genesis, Exodus, and Numbers.

to recognize Cuba. But at the same time they are completely preoccupied with them, like sneaking a whisper to an aide in the middle of dinner, "What are they doing now?" No doubt Pharaoh had his strategy for disposing of them or rendering them politically irrelevant or making them "inoperative," but they kept coming back. And you know that this population explosion that so scared the empire did not simply mean that they bred a lot. Rather, it means that the blessing of God was out there and not in here. And that raises questions for people who circumscribe the conditions of the meal, like why should they come in here with us if the blessing activity of God is out there with them? It is a hint that haunts everybody who is busy guarding the inside against the outsiders.

The Bible draws a conclusion from these two observations: (a) that insiders are blessed for the sake of outsiders, and (b) that the blessing is out there with them and not in here with us. The conclusion is announced in Exodus 3, all about the burning bush. The eternal voice of "Let-My-People-Go" (that is the name by which we may call God) will not accept "No shoes, no shirt—no service—no exceptions." God is restless with barring folks on the outside; and if it comes to that, as it often does, it just turns out that the action, vitality, and creativity are no longer found on the inside, but on the outside. It surely turned out that way that time. The power toward freedom surfaced among the Hebrews, not among the Egyptians. Indeed, there may be something constituent about Egyptians (read "insiders") that prevents freedom from surfacing among them. Imagine the gloomy mood in the palace with all their reports and quotas and staff meetings. All the forms of power and prestige, but the action—the really human action—is not in here, but out there. And the barriers we have set up, the restrictive signs on the doors, do not keep people out. Actually they block us insiders in.

Perhaps there is a message here about our ways of building institutions that judges and warns us all:

- We all know churches that try to control access to the Holy, who unpredictably breaks out somewhere else in healing ways, and we are bothered by the breakout.
- We are accustomed to modern medicine, with the development of high medical standards, strong medical institutes, and a powerful lobby of doctors and hospitals and insurance

companies, and then the idea comes that healing may be a folk art, which all that establishment can't administer.

- In our schools, all the way from kindergarten to graduate schools, we control access to learning, and we get de-schooling and the strange disillusionment of adults and kids who suspect that schools are not where one gets access to learning.

Now I do not mean to draw any radical conclusions about revolution and dismantling our institutions. Such a conclusion is beyond the text, and I think is nonsense. Ours is a more subtle point: Our power to organize and control is tenuous, and we may control only appearances, not power. The gospel is the affirmation that 'Let-My-People-Go may be kept out, but God can't be kept in, and perhaps our efforts to keep others out may just consign them to being where the healing action is.

From the affirmation "That is an abomination to the Egyptians," it is not a far step to this other poetic notion:

He had no form or majesty that we should look at him
    [let alone eat with him],
        nothing in his appearance that we should desire him.
[Shepherds and many others are repulsive.]
He was despised and rejected by others;
    a man of suffering....
and as one from whom others hide their faces
    he was despised, and we held him of no account.
        (Isaiah 53:2–3)

The shepherds increase. Holiness stirs even now among the old, the young, and the whole company of the disenfranchised whom we have excluded.

It is not different in the New Testament. Jesus, as remembered by Luke, is impressed with the symbolic power of eating, the primal way we order our existence, and our perceptions. Perhaps you always knew this text. I'm sure I did. But it just hit me recently, and it stirs me and terrifies me when I hear it. Listen to this:

"When you give a luncheon or a dinner, do not invite your friends or your brothers or your relatives or rich neighbors, in case they may invite you in return, and you would be repaid. But when you give a banquet, invite the poor, the crippled, the lame, and the blind. And you will be blessed, because they cannot repay you, for you will be repaid at the resurrection of the righteous." (Luke 14:12–14)

This is a staggering comment that catches most of the Lukan gospel in one instant.

The text is perfectly symmetrical with a "do" and a "do not." *DO NOT* invite all the insiders! And the reason? Because they will repay you. We have that conversation in our house. Let's don't invite them because we will get involved with them, and it goes back and forth, so let's stay clear of that. Jesus offers an alternative to burdensome social obligations. There is something gross and debilitating about living in a *quid pro quo* world where there are no unanswered gifts, no disinterested risks, no freely given suppers. Jesus also, in another place (Matthew 5:43–48), said, "If you love those who love you, what reward do you have? Do not even the tax collectors do the same?" Everybody lives in a safe, measured world where we get and give all on the same scale. But all those other neat things—surprise, newness, play, Sabbath—all of them cannot come into a perfectly symmetrical universe. We are reduced to calculation, and no humanness rises there. It is a no-surprise environment devoid of graciousness.

I have wondered what sign Jesus would have on his drive-in. He hints here that it might say, "No friends, no kinsmen, no rich neighbors—no exceptions." A hard saying indeed!

And then the counterpart: DO! And we have that whole repulsive list that includes everyone but Hebrews. But aren't they all Hebrews, the ones shut out whom God would liberate?

- The poor, people with no manners?
- The maimed, crippled bodies that fascinate and repel?
- The lame, their clubbed feet that irritate?
- The blind, so aggressive, loud, and presuming?

I want my little tea party, and they have no manners. There are two kinds of dinners, one symmetrical and one for folks who can't repay or reciprocate with an invitation. Each dinner yields its own brand of humanity—Pharaoh's kind of humanity and Jesus' kind. One is proper and exclusive, the other is on the move, vital, and healing. And then in good didactic fashion, Jesus' statement adds a motivational clause (verse 14): "You will be blessed, because they cannot repay you, for you will be repaid at the resurrection of the righteous *[sadiq]*." That's a good time for repayment, not by the poor and outcast, but by God. When the new humanity is born and the new creation is called into existence, you'll be there. And it won't be the same dull social obligation, but something like you never imagined. And you'll be there!

The same motif is at many places in Luke. He plays on the theme of humbleness and exaltation and invites some to go up higher to a place of honor at the dinner (Luke 14:7–11). He observes that the well-off usually don't come, and so the invitation is given to the unqualified because they just might come, not being so worried about propriety. This text is the other side of the passage in Luke 14:12–14 that we have considered. There Jesus says, "Don't invite them." Here he discerns that they won't come anyway, because this kind of party is not attractive to them. Jesus is clearly radicalizing the rules of society for giving parties, and in doing that he is tampering with the primal ordering of society. Clearly he is calling into question the vision of *shalom* that lies behind and within rules for banquets. It is important to recognize his radical critique and his incredible alternative. He is not just creating a new guest list, but he is offering a whole new vision of reality that dictates how parties are held. All of that is expressed in the condemnatory, harsh language of Luke 7:34: "Look, a glutton and a drunkard, a friend of tax collectors and sinners!"

And this condemnation is followed in the Lukan sequence by the most extraordinary presentation of our theme. The story is "at table." Jesus is the guest of a Pharisee, obviously one who cherished a symmetrical, no-surprise world. Then comes the surprise: a nameless woman off the street who is welcomed by Jesus, but quite unwelcomed by the symmetrical host. Jesus makes three unmistakable contrasts between outcasts and "incasts"—outcasts who are where the action is and in-casts who presume to control access to the goodies:

> "You gave me no water for my feet, but she has bathed my feet with her tears and dried them with her hair. You gave me no kiss, but from the time I came in she has not stopped kissing my feet. You did not anoint my head with oil, but she has anointed my feet with ointment." (Luke 7:44–46)

The conclusion is drawn. The symmetrical Pharisee who has access to the goodies won't get many, and indeed he has all he'll ever get. But the woman is saved and departs in *shalom*.

The Lukan presentation is much heralded as a gospel to the outcast, and that is correct—to the ones who have no shoes and no shirts and, therefore, get no service. The perfectly symmetrical person makes sure there are no exceptions, but the Lukan narrative pays attention to the folks who own all the drive-in franchises. They are obviously undone by the undoing of their social constructions of reality:

> The chief priests and the scribes were looking for a way to put Jesus to death. (Luke 22:2)

> But they were insistent and said, "He stirs up the people." (Luke 23:5)

And Pilate observes:

> "You brought me this man as one who was perverting the people." (Luke 23:14)

The received ones who are weary of being excluded hear Jesus gladly and accept the invitation promptly. They are the ones filled with amazement and perhaps gifts. But the others are obsessed with rules of propriety, and they are consumed with hardness of heart. It is put so well in Luke 19:47–48:

> The chief priests, the scribes, and the leaders of the people kept looking for a way to kill him; but they did not find anything they could do, for all the people were spellbound by what they heard.

This is not antiestablishment talk. Rather, it is a question to those who have leverage to order churches, families, clubs, committees, classrooms, worlds. It is the recognition that we choose our brand of order and must live with the blessings it can issue. The reward talk of Luke affirms that there is a context in which our *quid pro quo* rewards will not satisfy. And we must think about that, for we live in a culture that is heavily committed to *quid pro quo* rewards. But the assumption of Luke and of the church is that the human spirit cannot settle for that. It yearns for and must have gifts beyond rules, meals beyond qualifying exams.

But we do not always pay attention to how we eat and order our *shalom*. We find ourselves eating and drinking "in an unworthy manner" (1 Corinthians 11:27), not only at the Lord's table, but at all our tables, because we eat not for sharing but for ordering reality in an exclusionary way. And Jesus called all of that into question by ripping down our signs and giving access to all. This is what it means to say:

> "The blind receive their sight, the lame walk, the lepers are cleansed, the deaf hear, the dead are raised, the poor have good news brought to them." (Luke 7:22)

They all have access to the goodies because the old doorkeepers have been displaced.

Finally, out of Proverbs, that book for all seasons, is this on primal ordering at the table:

> Better is a dinner of vegetables where love is than a fatted ox and hatred with it. (Proverbs 15:17)

7

Peace Is a Gift and a Task

One who is often reproved, yet remains stubborn,
will suddenly be broken beyond healing.
When the righteous are in authority, the people rejoice;
but when the wicked rule, the people groan.
A child who loves wisdom makes a parent glad,
but to keep company with prostitutes is to squander one's
substance.
By justice a king gives stability to the land,
but one who makes heavy exactions ruins it.
Whoever flatters a neighbor
is spreading a net for the neighbor's feet.
In the transgression of the evil there is a snare,
but the righteous sing and rejoice.
The righteous know the rights of the poor;
the wicked have no such understanding.
Scoffers set a city aflame,
but the wise turn away wrath.
If the wise go to law with fools,
there is ranting and ridicule without relief.
The bloodthirsty hate the blameless,
and they seek the life of the upright.

87

A fool gives full vent to anger,
but the wise quietly holds it back.
If a ruler listens to falsehood,
all his officials will be wicked.
The poor and the oppressor have this in common:
the LORD gives light to the eyes of both.
If a king judges the poor with equity,
his throne will be established forever.

PROVERBS 29:1–14

It is clear that the church's usual theology of sin and forgiveness is not an adequate basis on which to think biblically about problems of international peace. It is obvious that the churches that historically have thought of sin, guilt, and forgiveness in a narrow sense have settled for a very individualistic articulation of the gospel. The narrow understanding of sin and forgiveness unfortunately provides no resources for thinking about public problems. I do not suggest that sin and forgiveness cannot be understood in relation to public issues. But it does not seem likely that any great effort will be made to give fresh articulation to those central biblical symbols. The individualistic way of thinking about the gospel came from a small, coping community—the early church—which, because of its size and position, could not have a major impact on public issues.[1] I am suggesting, then, that such a way of understanding the gospel ill-equips us to address our topic, namely, the biblical resources available to us in thinking through problems of peace and war. Moreover, it is clear that in our present context, the theological notions of sin, guilt, and forgiveness are fostered by establishment thinking in a way that assumes and encourages continuity of institutions and political, economic arrangements as they are. Talk of forgiveness

---

[1] It is clear that a major impetus toward articulating faith in terms of sin and forgiveness came from the priestly tradition, which achieved its full expression in the exilic period when such preoccupations seemed more urgent. On the priestly tradition, see especially Gerhard von Rad, *Old Testament Theology* 1 (New York: Harper and Brothers, 1962), 77–80, 232–79; and Frank M. Cross, Jr., *Canaanite Myth and Hebrew Epic* (Cambridge: Harvard University Press, 1973), 293–325. The dating of the tradition to the exile and setting it in the context of a community struggling for survival and identity does not, of course, deny the utilization of earlier materials, but the major impetus came precisely in the exilic period, when problems of identity were acute.

characteristically presumes the value and maintenance of things as they are. And surely this is supported and sustained by the persistent caricatures of faith and ministry in much of the mass media.

When we pay attention to large portions of scripture that do not concern themselves with sin, guilt, and salvation, we discover an important alternative model for thinking faithfully. Rather than focus on sin, guilt, and salvation, we will look at the concepts of chaos and order, that is, the problem of chaos and the powerful imposition of order as the divine resolution of the problem. It is a theme broadly rooted in the Bible, and a legitimate one for us precisely because the threat of chaos or *anomie* is all about us. Only a fool lacks at least a suspicion that the world is falling apart. So I raise the question of *shalom* in the Bible around this issue for ministry: How do we address *chaos?* And how do we celebrate order?

The biblical images for chaos are various. Some of them include the following:

The earth was a formless void, and darkness covered the face of the deep. (Genesis 1:2)

The waters swelled and increased greatly on the earth…The waters swelled so mightily on the earth that all the high mountains under the whole heaven were covered; the waters swelled above the mountains. (Genesis 7:18–20)

I looked on the earth, and lo, it was waste and void…
I looked, and lo, the fruitful land was a desert,
    and all its cities were laid in ruins. (Jeremiah 4:23a, 26)

He sustained him in a desert land,
    in a howling wilderness waste. (Deuteronomy 32:10)

From noon on, darkness came over the whole land until three in the afternoon. (Matthew 27:45)

These texts and others that could be added touch the decisive moments in the story of biblical faith. All kinds of traditions are represented. At least Genesis 1:2; 7:18–20 (and Isaiah 45:18–19) are royal in their origin. They intend to talk in the context of royal power, the legitimacy of royal power, and the terror that surfaces in the absence of royal power. And surely Matthew 27:45 is about kingship and what happens when it is removed from the social, cosmic scene.

If we are going to talk about peace, we have to make a fundamental decision about ourselves. How we make that decision will determine in large measure how we shall speak about theology. Narrowly preoccupied citizens can do theology around questions of sin, guilt, and salvation. That is an important task. But royal types, by which I mean people charged with resisting chaos and making peace, must not be preoccupied with those interesting but confining questions. Rather, theology must be done around the issues of freedom and power, authority and responsibility. And when those issues are faced squarely, we shall be speaking about peace. And when those questions are resolved, we shall be on the way to authentic *shalom.*

Order as Gift

So for royal types—and we are royal types preoccupied with chaos and order—theology must face the issues of freedom and power, authority and responsibility. It must ask about the imposition and management of order and the subtle, insidious ways in which chaos comes among us. Order, that is, the imposition of viable forms of life on the chaos around us, is both a gift and a task. To the extent that it is a gift, that is, the enduring work of God, we are relieved of anxiety. There are some things you can count on. The world will not fall apart. At the bottom of life are a confidence and buoyancy about the world. The world will not collapse, and we need not be frantic about the prospect that it will. This, I believe, is a dimension of reality lost in our time, impressed as we are with our capacity to make and unmake the world. Our pride about our capacity has led us to despair about our inability. Because we thought we could make and unmake worlds, we now are depressed with our failure to do so. Well, of course! The Bible believes that we cannot finally unmake the world because we have not made the world. There is a drive toward *shalom* located in the promises of God that we cannot obviate. The world is not at our disposal, and so we will not dispose of it for good or for ill. That is difficult for any modern folk to say because we are profoundly *homo faber.* But it is even more difficult and painful for people like us, prone to care in social action kinds of ways, because we are inordinately impressed with our responsibility and the burdens of our humanity.

But the witness of scripture is clear. We cannot make or unmake the world, because it is not ours:

1. This is the witness of the Sabbath: God rested![2] Think of the boldness of that statement. God rested. The One charged supremely with ordering the world was not in a tizzy about making it go. And the commandment is very clear: We rest because God did (Exodus 20:8–11). And God rested because the reliability of the world has been ordained by God and is not in doubt.

2. Jesus, in one of his more precious and provocative statements related to our concern, asserts: "Do not worry about your life…Can any of you by worrying add a single hour to your span of life?" (Matthew 6:25, 27). The world is whole and faithful enough that we need not be consumed in efforts to secure our own existence. It has been secured.

3. In his remarkable parable about the rich fool, and in the subsequent reflection on it (Luke 12:13–31), Jesus makes a shrewd intersection of "little faith," "coveting," and "worry." Underneath all three and common to all three is the assessment that the world will cohere only if we hustle to make it so. The gospel refutes such a desperate pretension. Order is a gift. The world is safe, and that calls for wonder, amazement, and gratitude. So the Westminster Catechism tradition is correct: Our chief end is to "glorify God and enjoy him forever." People who would care for peace can learn from Martin Buber's characterization of miracle, that it is any experience that leaves us with "abiding astonishment."[3] Abiding astonishment about the reliability of the world is a basis on which to reflect on the task of making peace. People who lack that sense of astonishment are likely to take themselves too seriously, and for them the world may finally become too anxious. Peace cannot come from anxiety, but only from confidence. So at the outset let us face the reality: order is *a precious gift from God.*

Order as Task

Having said that, it must also be affirmed that order is a *task entrusted to us.* There is work to be done. The drive toward well-being, which God has ordained in this world, is not self-actualizing and automatic. It must be shepherded and nurtured and, dare we say,

---

[2]I know of no more eloquent statement on the meaning of the Sabbath than that of Abraham Heschel, *The Sabbath and Its Meaning for Modern Man* (New York: Farrar, Straus, and Young, Inc., 1951). See also the discussion of Hans Walter Wolff, *Anthropologie des alten Testaments* (Munich: Kaiser Verlag, 1973), 200–10. Wolff discerns the sociologically revolutionary implications of Sabbath in Israel.

[3]Martin Buber, *Moses* (Oxford: Oxford East and West Library, 1946), 75.

even managed? And that, of course, is our opportunity and our problem. How do we seriously and competently manage the drive toward well-being that God has ordained without presuming, without possessing it, and without emptying it of its "gift" quality?

Israel is not the first to know that God's drive toward well-being must be managed. In the Greek tradition as far back as Hesiod, "The cosmic problem is to find the right form of authority."[4] The solution, of course, in both Israelite and Greek culture, and most times since, has been the institution of monarchy. Government exists to shepherd God's drive toward well-being, which is the mainspring of history. And while the ancient people characteristically devised monarchy, we may use the language of monarchy to refer to every apparatus of power—social, political, economic, religious—whatever form or under whatever legitimation.

In Israel's reflection on the human management of the divine drive, there is a great deal of confusion. The traditions on kingship do not all agree. At least one dominant tradition reads it this way: Israel, like every nation, was "tempted" to solve the order question by kingship, and Yahweh was perceived as not being eager for that solution. Of course, to use the word "tempted" is to stack the cards, but that is the nature of this tradition. So we should ask about that reading: How does kingship characteristically function? And the answer?

- It quickly and consistently becomes self-seeking (see 1 Samuel 8).
- It absolutizes itself and takes itself much too seriously.

The biblical evidence is extensive that the pretensions of absolutism are a characteristic mark of monarchy:

> He will punish the arrogant boasting of the king of Assyria and his haughty pride. For he says:"By the strength of my hand I have done it, and by my wisdom, for I have understanding; I have removed the boundaries of peoples, and have plundered their treasures." (Isaiah 10:12–13)

> Is this the exultant city
> that lived secure,

---

[4]See Mark K. Wakeman, *God's Battle with the Monster* (Leiden: Brill, 1973), 40, on the mythic dimensions of power in Greek understanding. Likely, the Israelite presentation is much more politically aware, but the issues are parallel—namely, to find forms of authority that will enhance rather than diminish the public good.

that said to itself,
"I am, and there is no one else"? (Zephaniah 2:15)

O Tyre, you have said,
"I am perfect in beauty." (Ezekiel 27:3)

Because your heart is proud
and you have said, "I am a god;
I sit in the seat of the gods,
in the heart of the seas." (Ezekiel 28:2)

Pharaoh king of Egypt,
the great dragon sprawling
in the midst of its channels,
saying, "My Nile is my own;
I made it for myself." (Ezekiel 29:3)

And perhaps most centrally, speaking of Babylon:

You said, "I shall be mistress forever,"
so that you did not lay these things to heart
or remember their end.
Now therefore hear this, you lover of pleasures,
who sit securely,
who say in your heart,
"I am, and there is no one besides me;
I shall not sit as a widow
or know the loss of children."
…You felt secure in your wickedness;
you said, "No one sees me." (Isaiah 47:7–8, 10)

These mock songs against some of the greatest nations in history
are, among other things, some of the best attempts to manage the
peace God has ordained in creation. Each of these great empires was
ready to take enormous responsibility. But each assumed, either early
or late, that it was subject to no law other than its own, blind to the
mystery in history, closed to the emergence of the healing, judging
word of God, which refuses to be domesticated.

And so the king became not an ad hoc arrangement but an
ontological principle by which the universe is ordered. No longer was

it one of many possible human forms of coping, but now it was the design of the gods. How could it be otherwise, if we pretend that order is only a task and not a gift, if we presume that the securing of well-being is left exclusively to us? If it is totally up to us, none but us, then we are all of it. The statement "There is no one besides me" may be not only a heady statement of freedom but also a desperate statement that there are no resources outside our own. The failure to concede graciousness and *shalom* in the structure of creation leads to a religion of works, a political theory based on anxiety, and an inevitable absolutizing of any structure that seems to work.

The logic is very clear. There is the easy passing from world order to national security, and a short step from national security to self-interest. If there is no order but the one we make, all things are possible. But more than that, we had better do something quick and firm. And to identify world well-being with national interest and self-interest is not an intentional lie. It may well be a self-deception made in good faith by desperate people who believe they are the only ones.

Thus, self-interest becomes state policy and, if we may say so, world strategy.

> You eat the fat, you clothe yourselves with the wool, you slaughter the fatlings; but you do not feed the sheep. You have not strengthened the weak, you have not healed the sick, you have not bound up the injured, you have not brought back the strayed, you have not sought the lost, but with force and harshness you have ruled them. (Ezekiel 34:3–4)

It didn't take much imagination to get to that point from 1 Samuel 8, and it surely establishes strong contrasts to the vision of Matthew 25:31–46.

What Israel came to see is that the very agent of *shalom* (the king) has become the chief benefactor of chaos.[5] The very one ordained either by God or by people to bring order has become the initiator of disorder. And in Jerusalem, as in Assyria, Babylon, and Egypt, and everywhere else, such royal government has become a highly organized form of chaos, "Because there is no one but me."[6]

---

[5]But see Walter Brueggemann, *Theology of the Old Testament: Testimony, Dispute, Advocacy* (Minneapolis: Fortress Press, 1997), 492–527.

[6]See especially the discussion of Robert McAfee Brown, *Religion and Violence* (Philadelphia: Westminster Press, 1973), in which there is a sensitive and subtle challenge to those of us who sustain establishment violence. The issues are very difficult, but the theological frame in which powerful people may ponder their power has to do with a theology of the cross, now articulated by Jürgen Moltmann and my former colleague M. Douglas Meeks.

Chaos—anticreation—need not be formless and anarchic. It can be highly ordered, intentional toward its goals. It can be simply graceless power that justifies everything in having its own way. Chaos presents itself as order. Death presents itself as life. Stones present themselves as fish. Demonic powers pose as agents of resurrection. And so kings, who are mandated for all things wholesome, can use their royal robes as masquerades for death and destruction. Helder Camara has powerfully exposed this in his discussion of institutional violence and repression, which pretends only to order and coherence.[7]

So, as Israel learned from the first day of monarchy, there are dangers in kingship, that is, in formal public ordering, but *shalom* is still the task of the king, which is to say that the power establishment has its legitimate work to do. The Bible, at least in most of its parts, is affirmative about the legitimate existence and function of ordering agents. But Israel has a peculiar notion of the right use of ordering power. It knows that kingship (government) is not ontological, that is, not ordained for itself as a center of reality. Kingship is always an incidental arrangement carved out of historical opportunity, always in the service of another ontological principle. We forget that about institutions as they become ends in themselves rather than servants and agents of a deeper priority. The biblical tradition and Israel in her reflection on monarchy are peculiar in affirming that the fundamental religiopolitical reality is not the king, but is Torah, not human distribution of power, but divine vision for society.[8]

Controlling the King

When we talk about chaos, order, and power, Israel very soon has to talk about Torah. It was a hard question then and is now to determine the relation of king and Torah, between officeholder and theological charter. Only once, in Deuteronomy 17:14–20, does Israel

---

[7]Helder Camara, *Spiral of Violence* (Denville, N.J.: Dimension Books, 1971). He refers to institutional violence as "establishment violence which attracts revolutionary violence" (30–31).

[8]In his analysis of religion and politics in Israel, George Mendenhall, *The Tenth Generation* (Baltimore: Johns Hopkins University Press, 1973), makes a contrast between the communal religious authority of the league and the monopoly of the monarchy: "It was the Mosaic period which constituted revolution; with Solomon the counter-revolution triumphed completely, only to collapse under the same weight of political tyranny and arrogance which had to do with the troubles of the pre-Mosaic period...The real issue was a fairly simple one: whether or not the well-being of persons is a function of a social monopoly of force, or the consequence of the operation of ethical norms, which are valued as determining the behavior of persons in society; whether to put faith in armies and armaments, or in the unpredictable Providence which guarantees the validity of the ethic—though not the reward...God is not an authority for political manipulation" (196–97). The important contrast is between religious risk and political manipulation. See especially chapters 7 and 8.

explicitly comment on that question.[9] And the task set for the king is surprising and perhaps doubtful. The king is to sit all day on his throne and read the Torah. And Torah, as you know, is talk about *mishpat* and *sedeqah*, about justice and righteousness. The monarchy is understood, valued, and legitimated according to the norms of Torah—justice and righteousness. The government, the forces of law and order, serve another notion of reality. The texts reflecting on this may be cited from a number of sources:

> Give the king your justice, O God...
> May he defend the cause of the poor of the people,
>   give deliverance to the needy,
>   and crush the oppressor...
> He has pity on the weak and the needy,
>   and saves the lives of the needy.
> From oppression and violence he redeems their life;
>   and precious is their blood in his sight.
>   (Psalm 72:1, 4, 13–14)

Wisdom speaking says:

> By me kings reign,
>   and rulers decree what is just;
> by me rulers rule,
>   and nobles, all who govern rightly...
> I walk in the way of righteousness,
>   along the paths of justice. (Proverbs 8:15–16, 20)

> By the blessing of the upright a city is exalted,
>   but it is overthrown by the mouth of the wicked.
>   (Proverbs 11:11)

> Like a roaring lion or a charging bear
>   is a wicked ruler over a poor people.
> A ruler who lacks understanding is a cruel oppressor;
>   but one who hates unjust gain will enjoy a long
>   life. (Proverbs 28:15–16)

---

[9]Gerhard von Rad, "Some Aspects of the Old Testament World View," in *The Problem of the Hexateuch and Other Essays* (New York: McGraw-Hill Book Company, 1966), 158–65, has set this text in a context where it can be understood as a protest against a "world-view that has become overweeningly presumptuous."

When the righteous are in authority, the people
rejoice;
but when the wicked rule, the people groan...
By justice a king gives stability to the land,
but one who makes heavy exactions ruins it...
If a king judges the poor with equity,
his throne will be established forever.
(Proverbs 29:2, 4, 14)

This is a radical and scandalous notion of power. Israel knows that choices are set in the context of inescapable givens, and the givens are created in the fabric of the world by the Lord who created and creates it. The fabric of the world itself is concerned with *mishpat* and *sedeqah;* they are the irreducible substance of *shalom.* They are the only path to order. And anything that resists this, no matter how arranged or contrived or disguised, is indeed chaos and must yield death.

Thus, the threat of the world falling apart, which is a concern both of ancient and modern folk, has been made into an ethical issue. The threat of chaos has become the abhorrence of injustice. The flood of chaos is now presented as an inundation of oppression. The prize example is, of course, Pharaoh in the exodus story, who, if he is anything, is the embodiment of order. But what an order— characterized by slavery, oppression, and coercion. Even if there are no riots and disruptions, that's not order; rather, it is closely and carefully supervised chaos. No wonder that in the retelling of the story of slavery and liberation, Pharaoh becomes the sea monster Rahab, chaos (Isaiah 30:7).[10] Yet a people is born out of this chaos. "The Most High himself will establish it" (Psalm 87:5). The order of *shalom* is not the contained chaos of the Pharaoh, but the justice and righteousness of the Lord. Because of this *shalom,* "Singers and dancers alike say, 'All my springs are in you'" (Psalm 87:7).

---

[10]Frank M. Cross, Jr., *Canaanite Myth and Hebrew Epic,* 112–44, has carefully explored the mythic dimensions of Exodus 15 as a way in which Israel used Canaanite rhetoric and images.

8

PEACE IS A *SHALOM* COVENANT

The heavens are telling the glory of God;
*   and the firmament proclaims his handiwork.*
Day to day pours forth speech,
*   and night to night declares knowledge.*
There is no speech, nor are there words;
*   their voice is not heard;*
yet their voice goes out through all the earth,
*   and their words to the end of the world.*
In the heavens he has set a tent for the sun,
*   which comes out like a bridegroom from his wedding canopy,*
*   and like a strong man runs its course with joy.*
Its rising is from the end of the heavens,
*   and its circuit to the end of them;*
*   and nothing is hid from its heat.*
The law of the LORD is perfect,
*   reviving the soul;*
the decrees of the LORD are sure,
*   making wise the simple;*
the precepts of the LORD are right,
*   rejoicing the heart;*

the commandment of the LORD is clear,
  enlightening the eyes;
the fear of the LORD is pure,
  enduring forever;
the ordinances of the LORD are true
  and righteous altogether.
More to be desired are they than gold,
  even much fine gold;
sweeter also than honey,
  and drippings of the honeycomb.
Moreover by them is your servant warned;
  in keeping them there is great reward.
But who can detect their errors?
  Clear me from hidden faults.
Keep back your servant also from the insolent;
  do not let them have dominion over me.
Then I shall be blameless,
  and innocent of great transgression.
Let the words of my mouth and the meditation of my heart
  be acceptable to you,
  O LORD, my rock and my redeemer.

PSALM 19

Israel discerned that the matter of *shalom* is a delicate balance of several factors:

- The gift of creation is not negotiable or at our disposal.
- The principles of *sedeqah* and *mishpat* found in the Torah cannot be compromised.
- The power of the ruler, sometimes presented as a grant of the people and sometimes as a grant of God, can be held arrogantly or exercised for the people.

Those components have not changed. We struggle to keep these affirmations in balance, and occasionally we think a different balance might yield more. We learn very slowly.

So *shalom* is the establishment of order, but a very strange order:

- It is not the order of *ontos*, in which everything is given and ordained by the gods.

- It is not the order of *techné,* in which everything is made by us and at our disposal.
- It is order in the hassle of covenant.[1]

Covenant has been a much used word in scripture study, but we have only begun to think carefully about what it means to perceive reality as covenantal. Covenant is many things. It includes the intentional affirmation of hurts and needs or resources and energies among agents who take each other seriously. It depends on the resolve of the establishment to be fully historical, that is, to make covenantal choices (choices for the other) in the midst of enormous pressures of human need and self-interest.

And as we have known for a long time, covenant makes us live with the terror and dynamic of historicality, that is, recognizing and living fully with and in the limits of human history. Rather than taking flights to meanings that are immune to relational precariousness, we have to live in the here and now with the real competing pressure of power firmly held. It is such historicality that invests choices with great seriousness but stops short of ultimacy. It is historicality that leaves us sensitive to healing delicacies in our use of power and the precariousness of all our choices and best plans. It is historicality that leaves us with fears and hopes and ambiguities and nowhere to run from them. It is historicality that leaves us free of the tyrannical givens and desperate drivenness. So to view life and our ways of ordering it covenantally is to live faithfully and seriously with brothers and sisters in all crunches of historicality. We are not free to go the sacral way of *ontos,* nor the profane way of *techné.* We must face up to the only kind of *shalom* worth having, that of our historicality. And, of course, every ruler, every agent of order, every entrenched voice of establishment wants to transcend historicality. But that is to deny covenant—to deface our brothers and sisters and to deny our own brotherhood and sisterhood.

Covenant as a way of *shalom* in a world of historicality requires at least three ingredients, if we take the memory of Israel seriously.

---

[1] The terms are those of Arend van Leeuwen, *Christianity in World History* (London: Edinburgh House Press, 1964). While his preference for *techné* over *ontos* appeared attractive at the time of his writing, much has happened to us since then. More recent reflection, heavily influenced by Jacques Ellul, suggests that either alternative—*ontos* or *techné*—is unacceptable. We must begin again with covenant.

First, covenant requires *an agent of order*, who in the Bible is characteristically the king, though it may be the government or the doctor or the teacher or the parent. It is the agency of legitimated authority, and the function of the king is clear—to arrange and administer power in the face of chaos so that people can be human after the image of God:

- to manage food so that people can eat
- to manage demons so that people can be free
- to manage sickness so that there can be health
- to address death in life-giving ways

Such a way of describing it gives us a fresh glimpse of Jesus. He did feed the people, and he dealt with the demons. He did heal, and he did overcome death. So he is then the real king and the model for how rulers and people with power are to conduct themselves. They exist for the community. The ruler exists for the people.

But if the ruler can transcend historicality (which Jesus refused to do [Luke 4:1–13] and so was crucified, the supreme moment of his historicality), then the ruler's notion of order is subject to none, may be questioned by none, is accountable to none, and must be defended at any cost. As we learned repeatedly in the late twentieth century, the U.S. presidency can easily become a convenient case in point, in which all kinds of behavior have been legitimated to "defend the presidency." From the perspective of its defenders, the office needed to be an eternal institution beyond historical accountability and therefore without the claims or demands of covenant.

Second, viable order and *shalom* require *an agent of vision*. In the Bible, the prophet is the agent of vision, the one who has no vested interest in the way things are, who has little effective power to change things, but who has caught the vision of a new land and new people in the new age. The prophet has a keen sense about who is really in charge. The prophet is seduced by no idolatry or self-interest.

Such an agent on which a society depends can speak of justice, which means care for the weak in the best interests of the weak. Such an agent can speak of holy power and holy purpose, both precious and precarious, which cannot be perverted. And most majestically such an agent can affirm the link between the two—justice for the poor and holy purpose and power. The prophet can dare to affirm that the practice of justice results in order, whereas the practice of injustice leads to chaos:

(Injustice)
>Swearing, lying, and murder,
>>and stealing and adultery break out;
>>bloodshed follows bloodshed.

(Chaos)
>Therefore the land mourns,
>>and all who live in it languish;
>together with the wild animals
>>and the birds of the air,
>>>even the fish of the sea are perishing.
>>>(Hosea 4:2–3)

(Injustice)
>Hear this word, you cows of Bashan...
>who oppress the poor, who crush the needy,
>>who say to their husbands,
>>>"Bring something to drink!"

(Chaos)
>...they shall take you away with hooks...
>Through breaches in the wall you shall leave,
>>each one straight ahead. (Amos 4:1–3a)

(Injustice)
>Hear this, you rulers of the house of Jacob...
>who abhor justice
>>and pervert all equity,
>who build Zion with blood
>>and Jerusalem with wrong!

(Chaos)
>...Zion shall be plowed as a field;
>Jerusalem shall become a heap of ruins,
>>and the mountain of the house a wooded
>>>height. (Micah 3:9–10, 12)

These are remarkable statements of coherence that link the practice of justice and the existence of order, or the practice of injustice and the emergence of chaos. Or, in Israel's categories, the honoring of Torah and the enhancement of creation. This agent of vision who sees things the ruler does not has the delicate task of holding together God's will for us, which concerns our obedience, and God's will for creation, over which we have no control.

The ruler thinks always about the ordering. The prophet thinks about Torah, which the ruler thinks does not matter. Torah is especially the giving of power to the powerless. It revives the soul, makes the simple wise, rejoices the heart, and enlightens the eyes. (See Psalm 19:7–8.) Torah is the reflection that creation is the Lord's, not ours, that it is not at our disposal, and that while demands are placed on us, no matter what our power we are not free to do what we will with our power in the place where we are. This is what the agent of vision must always say to the agent of order: We are not free to do what we will. Some demands are placed on us.

It hardly needs to be said, does it, that in the modern world, our world, we are big on agents of order and short on agents of vision? It has always been so. The agents of order control all the arms, all the hardware, and the agents of vision are often reduced to reciting poems people neither understand nor value. It is an uneven conversation, but agents of order and vision must listen to each other, or so Israel believed.

Although we cannot say that every community must have it, we can simply observe that every community has a third component: *those without power*—the poor, the excluded, the impotent, the disinherited, the repulsive whom we prefer not to see. In the Old Testament they are "widows and orphans." In the New Testament they are "publicans and sinners." Our own recital concerns the poor, the minority, the women, and the aged. Their identity really does not change much. They are the waiting ones who haunt the "haves." And surely how the agents of order and vision relate to each other determines how these folks fare.

Israel had a radical notion that these folks, the powerless, are destined to power. That, of course, is against all the data, and we choose not to believe it. But since the exodus, Israel has known the truth of it. The purpose of God is the empowerment of the powerless. This is what the agent of vision must say to the agent of order. Things will not be as they are. That is why it takes an agent of vision. The agent of order (king) is focused on how it is. The agent of vision (prophet) is to address how it is going to be. The agent of vision discerns the new to be wrought by the purposes of God, and must insist to the ruler that newness is coming. Things as they are will cease to be. And the change from what is to what will be concerns the powerless. The new thing God is doing is empowering them to full humanness.

When we talk about *shalom,* we must talk about the dynamics and interaction between these elements in the community:

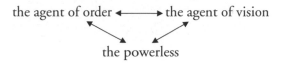

the agent of order ←——→ the agent of vision

the powerless

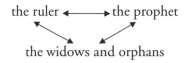

the ruler ←——→ the prophet

the widows and orphans

And when the ruler and prophet talk to each other, they must talk about the new that is to come, which means that the agenda is always about how the powerless will come to power.

In a *shalom community:*

- The ruler listens to the prophet and cares for the poor, because that is the office of a ruler.
- The prophet speaks boldly and constructively, knowing that the king intends to rule well.
- The powerless are coming into power.

In a *perverted community,* in which the power questions are not faced honestly:

- The ruler listens to no one, silences the prophet, and abuses the impotent for his or her own ends (1 Samuel 8; Jeremiah 22:13–17).
- The prophet is silenced because the king cannot tolerate the vision. (See Manasseh in 2 Kings 21:1–18.)
- The poor become for all practical purposes slaves (1 Kings 5:13; 1 Samuel 8).

Of course, we live in perverted communities. But we are not yet done insisting that *shalom* can come in our community. Rulers can listen and prophets can speak and the powerless can be honored. We believe that because of the primal events of our faith.

The exodus is precisely such an interaction:

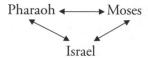

And the conclusion is that the slaves were freed and a new energy was loosed in history.

It is the same with the event of the resurrection:

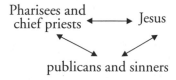

And the conclusion is that the dead one was raised and a new energy was loosed in history.

The making of peace is hard work because we are talking about basic modifications in the way we order our lives. But if we are to work at peace, it is essential that the agent of vision be present and potent in the face of the ruler. Every community is a tenuous arrangement of powers, and we must face the reality that every legitimate form of order is to some extent an expression of authorized violence calculated to keep the powerless out of control.

We should not be romantic about peace. *Shalom* is caused by and requires *interventions that will redistribute power. Shalom* depends on the redistribution of power. With people (the manipulators of hardware) nothing is possible. With God (the voice of the vision of newness) all things are possible (Luke 18:27). And sometimes power is shared, and folks are raised to life. And then angels sing of peace.

9

MIXING RELIGION AND POLITICS

Then all the elders of Israel gathered together and came to Samuel at Ramah, and said to him, "You are old and your sons do not follow in your ways; appoint for us, then, a king to govern us, like other nations." But the thing displeased Samuel when they said, "Give us a king to govern us." Samuel prayed to the LORD. And the LORD said to Samuel, "Listen to the voice of the people in all that they say to you; for they have not rejected you, but they have rejected me from being king over them. Just as they have done to me, from the day I brought them up out of Egypt to this day, forsaking me and serving other gods, so also they are doing to you. Now then, listen to their voice; only—you shall solemnly warn them, and show them the ways of the king who shall reign over them."

1 SAMUEL 8:4–9

Then Pharisees and scribes came to Jesus from Jerusalem and said, "Why do your disciples break the tradition of the elders? For they do not wash their hands before they eat." He answered them, "And why do you break the commandment of God for the sake of your tradition? For God said, 'Honor your father and your mother,' and, 'Whoever speaks evil of father or mother must surely die.' But you

107

*say that whoever tells father or mother, 'Whatever support you might
have had from me is given to God,' then that person need not honor
the father. So, for the sake of your tradition, you make void the
word of God. You hypocrites! Isaiah prophesied rightly about you
when he said:*

> *'This people honors me with their lips,*
> *but their hearts are far from me;*
> *in vain do they worship me,*
> *teaching human precepts as doctrines.'"*

MATTHEW 15:1–9

The issue of the delicate relation of faith and politics may be
located in two polarities, common to human experience, that are
concerns of both religion and politics.

The first of these polarities is *chaos and order.* Chaos, in a variety
of forms, is a source of anxiety and threat. It is experienced as
lawlessness in the community, as insanity in a person, in unexplained
upheaval and incoherence in every aspect of life. All of us scramble
and work hard to avoid the threat of chaos.

A major political concern, articulated most clearly by the
philosopher Thomas Hobbes, is to devise ways of controlling chaos,
of channeling energy into useful and manageable forms. It is surely
correct that political institutions are established to bring order to social
interaction, and economic arrangements to bring order to the exchange
and accumulation of goods and property. Order is to "ensure domestic
tranquillity."

Chaos is experienced in a variety of forms in the Bible. Cosmically
it is evident in the dark shapelessness before creation (Genesis 1:2,
echoed in Mark 4:35–41). It is recognized in the ominous upheavals
evoked by the death of Jesus (Matthew 27:51–54; Mark 15:33–39).
Historically, chaos is expressed as a situation in which everyone does
what he or she pleases (Judges 17:6; 18:1; 19:1), and, therefore,
everyone is a threat to everyone else. The stories of Judges 17—21 are
dramatic expressions of social chaos, which appears as base and
demeaning behavior, destructive of human values and human dignity.

In such a context, appropriate political action is to create
instruments of order. In the Bible, the principle of order is represented
by kingship. Monarchy exists to bring coherence and security to a
threatened community. In some cultures, kingship was viewed as a

part of the divinely structured arrangement for creation. Thus, when Israel was faced with historical anarchy, the people asked for a king, surely in desperation (1 Samuel 8:5, 20). Israel proposed to be ordered like every other nation because its own primitive forms of order had failed.

But Israel's proposals for kingship have an important peculiarity. Israel was clear and consistent in the recognition that the institution of monarchy was not part of a created order as though it had an external sanction. Rather, it was a freely made political choice, made by human persons to cope with a historical crisis, a factor of extreme importance for our theme.

The main thrust of the Bible is that no political arrangement has divine sanction, though a variety of forms may be legitimated as historical creations. The monarchy in Israel may have been approved by God, but it was evoked by history and was subject to historical limitation. Israel could not flinch from being political, that is, from creating agencies that could establish order and cope with chaos. And there is no doubt that monarchy dealt effectively with the problem, which in the first case was the Philistine threat. Because of an historical choice, *Israel was ordered.* Monarchy was the resolution of the chaos/order issue.

The close connection of order and king is indicated in texts such as 2 Samuel 15:30; 21:17; Lamentations 4:20. These various texts affirm that the person of the king and the institution he embodies are essential to holding the world together. In a very sophisticated form, the point is expressed in Colossians 1:17, "In him all things hold together."

The second polarity is *injustice and justice.* Justice, a major concern of the Bible, refers to securing and guaranteeing the livelihood, well-being, freedom, and dignity of every person in the community, not only those strong enough to insist on it. Thus, justice is not punitive or retributive, but means a guarantee of well-being to all. (Cf. Matthew 23:23, where it is linked with mercy and faith, and Hosea 2:19–20, in which it is related to the most important components of biblical faith.)

God on the Side of Justice

One of the crucial insights of the Bible is that God is on the side of justice, that God is concerned for the well-being of those who lack power to secure it. God is presented as aware that in the unrestrained process of social life, injustice will develop because some have more power than others and those with power will use their power to secure greater self-advantage at the expense of the less powerful and the powerless. If unchecked, the unequal distribution of power expressed as injustice will enhance some, while others are robbed of their dignity and well-being.

In a very old psalm (82:1–7), God is presented as the one who gives justice to "the weak and the needy," to those who lack power to do it for themselves. In this psalm, God is sharply contrasted with the other gods, who "judge unjustly and show partiality to the wicked." In Psalm 99, God is described as the "lover of justice," who establishes equity, presumably against the natural tendency of social interaction to establish inequity. The conviction that God is peculiarly interested in justice, in the humane treatment of all persons regardless of their power to secure it for themselves, is a crucial element for biblical faith, and one central to our position on political and economic questions.[1]

The prime dramatic evidence for this commitment of God is, of course, the exodus. There is a mighty confrontation at the beginning of the biblical story between Moses, who speaks God's concern for justice and freedom, and Pharaoh, who embodies the arrangement of order. As we know, the act of bold social action on the part of Moses resulted in freedom for Israel and the defeat of Pharaoh. Dramatically we see royal order (embodied in Pharaoh) called into question by divine concern for justice (articulated by Moses). Clearly the Bible celebrates justice at the expense of order. It is the exodus more than any other thing that determines how the Bible understands God. God is praised as one "who executes justice for the orphan and the widow, and who loves the strangers" (Deuteronomy 10:18).

In this regard, the God of the Bible is contrasted with all other gods. The pagan gods are generally friends of the kings, who are their patrons, and the gods legitimate and support whatever order happens to be in effect. By contrast, Yahweh, the God of the Bible, is no friend to order, but insists on justice and is ready and able to intervene in decisive ways, against legitimated order if necessary, to establish justice.

---

[1]Cf. Walter Brueggemann, *Theology of the Old Testament: Testimony, Dispute, Advocacy* (Minneapolis: Fortress Press, 1997), 234–35.

If God must choose between order and justice, God characteristically chooses justice.

Thus, we have suggested that two biblical events illustrate the issues before us. The narrative of 1 Samuel 8 shows Israel seeking a king for the sake of order. The narrative of the exodus shows God intervening for the sake of justice against the royal order of Pharaoh. Our analysis up to this point suggests that these two events, *establishment of kingship* and the *liberation story,* give shape to a pervasive problem in the Bible that is the core of our question.

One represents the *chaos/order* question. The other concerns *injustice/justice.* Our concern is to explore the tricky ways in which these two issues are related to each other. It is clear that both *order* and *justice* are important. Both are valued by God, and both are taken seriously in the Bible. Both are important to human experience, and both pose urgent contemporary questions. Concerning their relation, the Bible makes other affirmations:

1. Order and justice are not the same. It is a common mistake to assume that order, simply because it is established, is an adequate representation of justice. But it is clear that the king is the agent of order. The prophets (after the manner of Moses) are the agents of justice. At times prophet and king may agree, but many times they perceive things differently and, therefore, urge very different responses.

2. Order may be healing, but it also may be unjust. The Pharaoh's magnificent order in Egypt was just plain slavery; but from the perspective of the court circles, it was surely *orderly* slavery. And when Israel introduced royal order, it was reminded of the perverted, oppressive forms that order might take (cf. 1 Samuel 8:10–18). Some did not want to listen. Israel chose its form of social order knowingly but did not at that time worry about its being unjust, because the threat of chaos was immediate.

3. In a healthy political economic order, a king may act justly. Israel had a view of how this might work:

May he judge your people with righteousness,
    and your poor with justice…

May he defend the cause of the poor of the people,
    give deliverance to the needy,
    and crush the oppressor…

He has pity on the weak and the needy...
From oppression and violence he redeems their life.
(Psalm 72:2, 4, 13–14)

Justice here is understood as a positive and aggressive action. It has nothing to do with punishment or with the simple maintenance of established order. Rather, it is active intervention to transform society. And that transformation means, on the one hand, to act favorably toward the weak and, on the other hand, to act effectively against the abusive wrong. Thus, political institutions exist for the sake of active, transforming intervention if they are to do the will of God, who legitimates them.

4. Order can be perverted to be self-serving, to feathering one's own nest. Israel was not naïve, and the people discovered that when Israel did pervert justice, it brought destruction not only on those it was supposed to serve, but on itself:

Are you a king
    because you compete in cedar?...

But your eyes and heart
    are only on your dishonest gain,
for shedding innocent blood,
    and for practicing oppression and violence...

With the burial of a donkey he shall be buried.
(Jeremiah 22:15, 17, 19)

Such a political instrument is not ordained by God and cannot count on God's protection or legitimation. It emerged by historical choice and it will be destroyed or transformed by historical choice.

5. When *royal order* conflicts with *God-willed justice,* order must yield to justice, even if that creates a situation of disorder. God will risk chaos (as in the case of the exodus) to bring justice out of an unjust order.

The Bible, of course, is not blind to the ways in which our vested interests shape our perceptions. Every political and economic arrangement inevitably favors some and abuses others. Those favored normally and not surprisingly view the order as good, legitimate, and ordained by God. Those disenfranchised by the arrangement typically and not surprisingly view it as bad, illegitimate, and exploitative. And the issues of social action in the church depend on where the church places itself in regard to a given political-economic order: as legitimate and to be defended, or as exploitative and needing to be transformed. Kings (which means well-off people) tend to the former view; prophets (which means voices of radical faithfulness) tend to the latter.

Bible Biased toward Those Craving Justice

Historically there is no doubt that biblical faith emerged from the exploited and disenfranchised. Israel delivered from Egypt was a rejected, devalued slave population. Israel's taking the promised land was the landless taking the land away from the well-off. Thus, the bias of the Bible is toward those who crave justice, even if it means calling order—even royal order—into question.

Now, however, at least in American Christianity, we are an affluent people who benefit from the way the cards are currently stacked. We view present political and economic arrangements as good, so we live with the uneasy reality of a gospel that tends to be at odds with our vested interests. We are more naturally sympathetic to rulers who must wield power and guarantee order and manage quite complex decisions. But the Bible, our sacred book, represents a prophetic challenge. It protects us against royal order that masquerades as having divine approval.

I am aware that I have made the case from the Old Testament. But let us see Jesus in the context of these issues. Jesus' popular and more effective ministry was among those who for one reason or another were shut out, excluded from the benefits of the system. In the New Testament, Jesus fed the hungry, healed the sick, freed the demon-possessed. These are not to be understood as simple acts of compassion, but as dramatic challenges to a system that had deprived some of food, cut some off from health, and denied some their humanness. What all these outcasts had in common was their failure to honor the law. And those who did not honor the law could not get good jobs or positions of influence; nor could they enter the holy place. They were cut off from access to God and to human well-being.

It was the law, the principle of order, that excluded them. And the benefactors of that law, represented by the chief priests, scribes, and Pharisees, viewed the law as God-given and eternally ordained.

Jesus came into conflict with them on behalf of the poor. He exposed their law as a human device for manipulating power for the benefit of some and the disadvantage of others (Matthew 15:1–20; 23:1–36). Jesus' critique of the law was not made because the law was bad religion, but because it was used in the service of self-seeking politics and self-serving economics.

Notice the different reactions to Jesus' ministry. On the one hand, he was gladly received by the disenfranchised, who saw him as a powerful intervenor on their behalf:

> And a large crowd followed him and pressed in on him. (Mark 5:24)

> And the large crowd was listening to him with delight. (Mark 12:37)

> The crowd was pressing in on him to hear the word of God. (Luke 5:1)

These same people rejoiced and were amazed. Now what caused that? Clearly they perceived that he was taking action that would transform their situation. He did not simply talk; he acted. And his action was to deny the pattern of privilege and exclusivism that was at the heart of the political/economic and also the religious order of the day. Thus, Jesus carried on the prophetic protest against a system of order that legitimated injustice.

And, of course, Jesus evoked a passionate response from the guardians and benefactors of that order, who neither rejoiced nor were amazed. They were simply scared:

> The Pharisees went out and immediately conspired with the Herodians against him, how to destroy him. (Mark 3:6)

> But they were filled with fury and discussed with one another what they might do to Jesus. (Luke 6:11)

> Then the chief priests and the elders of the people gathered in the palace of the high priest, who was called Caiaphas, and they conspired to arrest Jesus by stealth and kill him. (Matthew 26:3–4)

The two groups and opinions are placed in juxtaposition in this statement:

When the scribes and chief priests realized that he had told this parable against them, they wanted to lay hands on him at that very hour, but they feared the people. (Luke 20:19)

Embodiment of an Unjust Order

The scribes and priests are the embodiment of an unjust order. The "people" are the victims of that order and yearn for justice, which they see in Jesus. The opposition to Jesus did not mobilize because he was an offensive rabbi, but because he took action that called into question the political/economic order of the time. He healed on the Sabbath, which violated both the precious Sabbath law and the social idea that the sick (outcast) people should stay in their place (Luke 6:6–11). He evoked opposition by an enigmatic statement that seemed to question governmental claims (Mark 12:13–17).

It was precisely Jesus' freeing, liberating actions on behalf of the victims of injustice that evoked the anger of the champions and benefactors of order. Jesus' ministry and his proclaiming of the intervening kingdom of God placed him squarely between these two groups, that is, the place at which social action must take place. In intervening at this place, he was faithful to the God of the exodus, who in the same way intervened for the freedom of the slaves against the oppressive order of Pharaoh.

It is neither legitimate nor necessary to read the gospels as class conflict narratives nor to define Jesus simply as a societal revolutionary. Obviously the narratives are more than this, and obviously the significance of Jesus is too great to be caught up in any single role or label. But the evidence does require us to see that the old conflict of justice and order, the long conflict of kingly legitimacy and prophetic protest, continued into the New Testament. Jesus presented himself and was understood by the early church as God's intervention to transform effectively or destroy the social powers, practices, institutions, and ideologies that dehumanized.

To Transform or to Destroy

Jesus offered two choices: to transform or to destroy. Like every prophet after Moses, he was unimpressed with the claims of legitimacy made by the institutions of order. Because God is Lord, Jesus believed that the only claim to legitimacy was the service of justice and well-being. This does not mean that he was an anarchist. He was not for chaos, but believed unjust political and economic arrangements were falsely legitimated embodiments of chaos. They had to end. Thus, his fundamental announcement of the coming of the kingdom (Mark 1:15) was an announcement that every agency that does not square with God's will for justice must change (repent) or be destroyed (judged).

The crucifixion/resurrection theme is the ultimate statement in the drama. Palm Sunday is the moment of dramatic confrontation when Jesus entered the city of Jerusalem, the city of legitimated order, and confronted the other rulers with the claim of God's rule. Good Friday is the vindication of privileged order. The leadership of the day silenced him; they remained in charge. But something enormous happened. Their order was pitiful and ineffective, and was shaken by earthquake (Matthew 27:51–54). The order endured, but the earth was falling apart. And decisively, Easter was the establishment of God's rule over all of life, including institutions that determine the parameters of our humanness. In Jesus' decisive action, the kingdom of this world was transformed into the kingdom of God. That was the point of his intervention into the affairs of his society.

The issues are complex, and conclusions are not easily drawn that will directly apply to today's situation. All of us have biases and convictions, depending on our background, our situation, and our vested interests. But some things seem clear:

- The biblical God in both Testaments is on the side of justice, even if it means protest against existing order.
- The prophetic protest against the kings is a continuous affirmation that God's will for justice cannot be voided. God's way will be done! (See Isaiah 2:6–22; 14:24–27.)
- Jesus effectively intervened to transform situations so that people could be more human.
- Jesus calls the church to share his ministry, to die with him for the sake of humanness, and to rise with him in power. Thus, he shares with his church his capacity to intervene and transform (Matthew 10:5–10; Luke 10:17–20).

After all those glorious affirmations, there are still our vested interests. We read the Bible and hear the gospel as our position permits us. As the law of God was used in the New Testament to protect positions of privilege, so a safe, domesticated, privatized gospel has its uses today. But the call to repent from such a safe faith persists.

Social action has had bad press, but it is to be understood as the continuing intervention of God to transform situations of order into situations of justice. It consists in a variety of strategies in an attempt to evoke repentance in our ideologies and our institutions. If the church is indeed the "body of Christ," then his body must run the risks of intervening to transform the places of injustice.

What is at issue is not whether we shall do this or that, but whether God's will for justice will effectively transform social institutions that tend to serve other purposes. It could happen that the time of the kingdom is at hand, when all kingdoms yield. One never knows.

PART FOUR

The *Shalom* Church

10

THE CHURCH: AN UNTANGLED WORLD

"I have said these things to you while I am still with you. But the Advocate, the Holy Spirit, whom the Father will send in my name, will teach you everything, and remind you of all that I have said to you. Peace I leave with you; my peace I give to you. I do not give to you as the world gives. Do not let your hearts be troubled, and do not let them be afraid. You have heard me say to you, 'I am going away, and I am coming to you.' If you loved me, you would rejoice that I am going to the Father, because the Father is greater than I. And now I have told you this before it occurs, so that when it does occur, you may believe. I will no longer talk much with you, for the ruler of this world is coming. He has no power over me; but I do as the Father has commanded me, so that the world may know that I love the Father. Rise, let us be on our way."

JOHN 14:25–31

The vision of *shalom* vis-à-vis the world is one that has troubled and dazzled the church since the beginning. The very earliest church

121

worked hard on that question. The church was fearful of the world because it was so big and hostile and resistant to the gospel, so possessed by demons and alien spirits. It is romantic to call the world our mission field, because it isn't exactly waiting to be "won over." And the image I get from the early church's memory is of a small, cringing community quiet in the waiting, waiting and listening, shivering at every siren and nearly fainting at every rap at the door. The world, then and now, is so big and fast, so powerful, so knowledgeable, and so formidable. And our church tradition is that the care of the world belongs to the heart of our faith.

The Fourth Gospel, in the farewell address of Jesus, provides some clues about how to think about this big world in relation to this little church. It is the affirmation of Jesus that "the ruler of this world is coming" (John 14:30). Now, this refers to no historical person or institution but, rather, to the destructive, demonic energies loose in our world, ranged against our humanness. How shall we speak of that threatening energy? In traditional language it is the devil; in the mythic language behind the Bible it is chaos. In more contemporary experience it is the driving power of greed and fear and manipulation. But we are not speaking simply of values. We are talking about values that have become objectified so that they have a claim on our lives—values that seem to act on our lives to compel us and coerce us to do what we would not and to be whom we would not choose to be. The ruler of this world is indeed coming. His name is Legion; he is all those coercing values that rob us of our freedom and deny to us the dignity and self-worth that is our inheritance from God. The ruler of this world has enormous power and momentum. His influence is impressive, and we are likely to be intimidated, if not seduced, by him.

But Jesus in his understated comments to his people says this: "He has no power over me" (John 14:30). That surely is gospel. The forces of antihuman, callous self-seeking have no power or legitimate claim over Jesus Christ—and, therefore, none over his community. That, of course, is what was going on in the last days of his ministry, as in the first days (Luke 4:1–13). After the frustration of the early days, the ruler of this world "departed from him until an opportune time" (Luke 4:13). And that time seemed to be in the last days of Jesus' life. In those days—beginning, end, and we may presume all the days between—the issue was to determine whose person he really was. The power of his faith was to determine that he was God's person and did not belong to this world. And because we are "in Christ," we may share the affirmation "He has no power over me." The little community of *shalom* is free, as the world is not. We are not victims of the power of greed and fear and manipulation and oppression and competence, all those powers that daily beset and beguile the world. The contrast is clear and dramatic: the big, impressive world enslaved, and the little, unimpressive community free. It is precisely the "towel" of empowering vulnerability that frees us (see John 13:1–17). And when we think about our faith and the "whole earth," this is an important affirmation to make. We owe nothing to the values of the world, and because we are not attracted to them, the gods of this age have no claim on us. We do not live in response to them! Hallelujah!

Jesus promised his little community so much. It prompted one of his disciples, either amazed or bewildered, to ask: "How is it that you will reveal yourself to us, and not to the world?" (John 14:22). It is a surprising choice Jesus made. This little people rather than that great company? This weak people rather than all those strong ones? This poor people rather than all those rich ones? God did indeed choose what is foolish, weak, poor, and despised (1 Corinthians 1:27–28). It is strange that God settled on that folk. It was a foolish choice, but one to be treasured among us. God Almighty appeared to us, not to the rulers of this world.

What is it God has promised that the world does not know? Simply that which separates the followers of Jesus from the slaves of this world—suffering love. This little, seemingly powerless community is ordered and identified by its practice of caring, transforming, empowering love of the towel-and-basin variety.

Roger Shinn said we live in a "tangled world."[1] But this little community consists of those who have gotten themselves untangled from the values of the world. We are not like the others. Our perception of the world is different, and because we see differently, we can both act and believe differently.

Does it surprise you that something happens to us when we are untangled from the values of the world? It is a hard question now whether or not one can even survive untangled. Peter Berger et al.'s book *The Homeless Mind* gives the painful suggestion that we have no alternative.[2] We must live tangled lives if we live at all. But this

---

[1]Roger Shinn, *Tangled World* (New York: Charles Scribner's Sons, 1965).

[2]Peter L. Berger, Brigitte Berger, and Hansfried Kellner, *The Homeless Mind: Modernization and Consciousness* (New York: Random House, 1973) shows how the props of modernity, technology, and bureaucracy have built a resistance toward untangling our lives.

community is given an alternative. This community is given the distance and perspective, the freedom and the energy to face the truth that the world does not suspect and cannot tolerate. We have that promise that "he will guide you into all the truth" (John 16:13). Pilate was not the last one who asked, "What is truth?" People are haunted that the world may be about something they don't understand; or worse, they are haunted that the world may not be about anything. But surely it is clear that the world is not about what we had assumed, and all those presumed values are placed in question.

The truth is given to a community that has the "towel" of empowering vulnerability. And, indeed, the suggestion is clear that only such a community may know the truth. We know something about the world that the world does not know about itself. That doesn't mean we have the right doctrine or the right morals, but that we can see clearly and know honestly how it is from the perspective of the hope-giving Lord. So what do we know in our "towel" community that the world cannot face about itself? Some things are obvious:

- We know that persons are more precious than property.
- We know that human worth is more precious than ideology.
- We know that quality is more important than quantity.
- We know that community-building can't be based on selfish advancement.
- We know that when we take our rules too seriously, we will crush or be crushed.
- We know that being able to do something (having a skill or capacity) doesn't automatically give it legitimacy, as, for example, with sex, or bombing, or hating, or developing.

We also know

- that this world is on its way out and no one can prevent that.
- that a new world is being given to humans and we are invited to it.
- that the movement from this world to the next is not made with full hands, but requires empty hands.
- that sorrow will be turned to joy while the world grieves.

Jesus summed it up so in his towel:

For all who exalt themselves will be humbled, and those who humble themselves will be exalted. (Luke 14:11)

That is the truth of the matter. Perhaps it is too much to claim that this is "all the truth," but it does come near the whole truth that Jesus embodied and taught. The whole truth by which Jesus lived and by which the church is invited to live does not consist of some obvious values commonly believed. It is, rather, a radical rejection of what the world knows and believes and a radical affirmation of what is absurd from the perspective of the world. The truth into which the church is led by the dying one is that the world is being dismantled, and a new world with a quite different code of operation is at hand. It is this dismantling that the church knows about and that the world has not yet begun to suspect; the world is too preoccupied and self-indulgent and so is not "grieved over the ruin of Joseph" (Amos 6:6).

In the church, we do not value and celebrate enough the precious perception we have been given of the world and of the world to come. That majestic truth is so simple and clear that we wonder at the fact that others do not see it. But seeing clearly depends on being untangled from the values of the world; only then can we perceive things after the perception of Jesus.

When the church sees the truth the world does not suspect and cannot bear, and when the church bears witness to this truth of dismantling and newness, the unequivocal result is asserted: The world hates the church. Jesus says, "If the world hates you, be aware that it hated me before it hated you." Now that is the bind we are in. The world wants *shalom;* but we know the world cannot have *shalom,* cannot possibly have it, on the present terms. The emergence of *shalom*—wholeness for church, people, and earth—requires some radical changes in values, presuppositions, and perceptions. *Shalom* happens only for communities engaged in empowering vulnerability. The world hates and resists those who speak of the dismantling required for *shalom.* The dismantling is required by the recognition that we cannot receive what we crave on the present terms. The world hates those who say such things as the following:

- You can't get peace by a policy of war.
- You can't get public tranquillity by a policy of discrimination in any form.
- You can't have happiness in society as long as women and children are seen as second-class citizens.
- You can't have self-respecting persons on the basis of self-seeking law and order.

Not to have *shalom* on terms we want is tough to take. But Jesus knew the things that make for *shalom*. He calls us friends and shares with us the makings of *shalom*, and that's fine for the beloved community. But the world will work hard to eliminate the very message about *shalom* that is our ministry. So from the beginning it has been clear: A church that cares about *shalom* can expect to be in conflict with a world still hoping that another way is possible.

But we know more than that we are friends in Jesus' purposes. We also believe the incredible promise that our "pain will be turned into joy" (John 16:20). The church is urged to reflect on the peculiar character of the pain, suffering, and hurt that it will experience for the beloved vision. The pain it will know is not pain to death; the hurt is not to endings and to closure. Life is not a cul-de-sac in which we are left to grieve. Rather, it is pain to new life. The image of hurt is that of labor pains, as with a woman in labor to bring forth a new life. The language strains to express the bursting of new life out of the midst of the agony that has some of the features of death agony— only it is life agony. So the images tumble:

- joy that a child is born into the world
- joy that no one can take from you
- joy that precludes doubts and uncertainties
- joy that is full

Newness is about to burst into our lives and, indeed, into the world. But the newness comes not without a price, and the price is death to all present arrangements, death to fear and to small hopes, death to old visions and to memories. And those who are ready for death to all that the world calls "life" are the ones to whom life can come. The world that will hate us does not know about joy; it knows about management and security and competence and stability, but none of that can yield joy.

And this statement about pain turning to joy ends in a most curious way:

"The hour is coming, indeed it has come, when you will be scattered, each one to his home, and you will leave me alone. Yet I am not alone because the Father is with me." (John 16:32)

And then Jesus adds: "I have said this to you, so that in me you may have *peace*" (John 16:33). There is our word! He has announced the scattering and the abandonment in order to have *shalom*. How could scattering and abandonment yield *shalom?* In this perhaps, that even though his "friends" are scattered and even though he is abandoned, he is with God. Does this not suggest that *shalom* for the church as for Jesus is discerned in the assurance that God is abidingly present? *Shalom* comes not by the norms of the world, nor through the acceptance of the world, nor by the reduction of its hostility. All of that can go on, and surely will. But the church is called to turn its appeal away from the world to God, to look only to God's presence for safety, to God's blessing for joy. Put simply, Jesus invites his friends to cast their lot as he has done on the single support of the faithful God.

The vision of the church is, therefore, very different from the vision of the world. The world is defensive because it believes things must be as they are. The world is grim because at best it is in a desperate holding action to keep things from deteriorating. But our vision is different. We do not fear the turn in the world because we know God's will for *shalom* will win out. We know God's vision of justice and wholeness will win out, and so we need not be fearful or grim as the world is. We can wait expectantly and not fearfully because we do not doubt that God's purposes for the world will win out. The church is left free to risk for *shalom* because we are sure of its coming. God's *shalom* is on the way because Jesus has declared it so, and we can move confidently toward the world that God will bring in good time. That is why we say at the communion table, "We proclaim the Lord's death until he comes." When he comes, he comes with power, power to fulfill all his promises. And rather than resist his promises, we trust ourselves to them and find ourselves free.

The issue drawn in this text by that fearful community in the face of the crucifixion is that the church perceives things as the world does not. But we must be honest enough to say of ourselves that both the church and the world are here with us today. Both the church with its vision and the world with its fear are here today, and they are in our guts. I am tangled up with the values and priorities of the world, and so are you; it cannot be otherwise. Part of the hatred of world toward church is within my own body and within yours. It has to do with the coerced parts of my person in conflict with the vision of joy that sustains me. And that conflict tears at me. We are all of us making up our minds about that deep conflict between yearning for *shalom* and wanting business with the world to continue uninterrupted. You and I will not likely rush madly to that new vision of confidence, but it is possible for folks like us to keep the tension alive. In the midst of a relevant, actionist church, it is useful for us to ponder what it means to be *in* but not *of* the world, *in* but not *of* the grimness and defensiveness, *in* but not *of* the joyless holding action. Or turn it around: *of* but not yet *in* the kingdom of the beloved, *of* the vision of a healed future but not yet *in* it. We do not have to be controlled by our *in,* but can be claimed by that which we are *of.* The struggle for the church, if it takes society seriously, is to get its *in* and its *of* very clearly in tension with each other.

Those of us in the church need to face the meaning of our heritage and destiny. We belong to a church that has chosen to live precisely in the "in/of" tension. Some people resent that ambivalence and give up on it. Some just endure and burn. Some embrace it and find their faith growing. But let us at least give thanks that we belong to a church tradition that knows something of in-ness and of-ness and is willing occasionally in important ways to face the hatred of the world in its grim defensiveness. We are committed to a whole earth of *shalom:*

- We have a hint that a society that wants to celebrate humanness will have to face the question of true amnesty in some healing ways.
- We have a hint that a society wanting just laws and stable order will have to get at problems of economic and political *inequality.*
- We have a notion that every human person is a *neighbor,* even the ones in need, and so we talk of "neighbors in need."

The big, difficult issues in the church are not this or that particular social action. More basically, the issue is the gospel affirmation that the world will be turned, meaning that some valued things must end and some feared things must begin. And when the world is turned, our little systems are called into question. We shall not all agree, ever, on any important issue. But it is time for all of us to face this amazing conviction: God has shown us the truth about *shalom,* and when we act on it, we are hated for it. We practice caring for the whole earth not because it is popular or bound to succeed, not because we are liberal or communist or whatever, but because we have faced a compelling vision of *shalom*. It's powerful tricky, but we can no more settle for a grim holding action.

Shalom is not only an incredible gift; it is a most demanding mission. But the world that will hate us as we seek its well-being is the same world that the Christ has already conquered (John 16:33). So we proceed with the confidence that the ruler of this entangling world has no power over us.

11

NEWNESS:
THE CHURCH'S MESSAGE

And the one who was seated on the throne said, "See, I am making all things new." Also he said, "Write this, for these words are trustworthy and true."

REVELATION 21:5

The gospel is about the coming of newness into our situation. It has been so since our mother Sarah got the word that she would have a child (Genesis 18:1–15). And news of pregnancy always means a radical change in perception, whether it is long-awaited, welcome news, or confirmation of one's worst fears. It was newness that night our fathers and mothers left Egypt, presumably on the way to the promised land, but in fact on their way to a waterless, meatless desert. And it was so every time Jesus came into the life of a person or a community. Wherever he was and to whomever he spoke and whomever he touched, things were new. That's what Jesus is like and what the gospel is about.

The world does not believe in newness. It believes that things must remain as they are. And for those of us who are well-off, it is a deep hope that things will remain as they are. Every new emergent is quickly domesticated; and if it cannot be domesticated, it is outlawed or crushed.[1]

That is the bite in our faith and the crunch in our ministry. We are bearers of newness. But we address and, in part ourselves constitute, a world that has a low tolerance level for newness. Yet the faith community, synagogue and church, exists precisely to announce the new, to affirm that we do not live by what is, but by what is promised. So the hassle goes on:

- *Kings* are always consumed with what is. There is from time to time a careful or frantic rearrangement of the parts, but always the same parts, and the rearrangement is limited and by design.
- *Prophets,* by contrast, are people who take seriously what is not yet so because they know something enormous is about to break in on us, something able both to tear apart and to heal.[2]

Or to take another word pair:

- *Technicians* work at relating resources and needs, so that life becomes the keen skill of problem solving. This should not be minimized in its importance. But it is not the route to newness, for technicians have as their business to predict and thereby to control. And where life is controlled, real newness does not and cannot come. Even Jesus encountered this, in a situation of unbelief, of resistance to expectation. He could do nothing powerful (Mark 6:5–6).
- *Poets* (not the people who make rhymes) are discerners of newness, people who fashion images for hopes that have not yet become visible, who sense the deep undertow of life and welcome it, who present to us images of reality that are expectant and expansive, who are content to receive what they

---

[1]Peter L. Berger, Brigitte Berger, and Hansfried Kellner, *The Homeless Mind: Modernization and Consciousness* (New York: Random House, 1973), 201–30 has shown how countercultural initiatives are given only so much room and then are domesticated into the system. Indeed, the analysis suggests little possibility that the dominant culture can be "countered," surely not with the social, political options the book considers. Perhaps it can be countered by nothing less than the radical gospel of the crucified One.

[2]This is nowhere clearer than in Jeremiah with the dominant theme, "to pluck up and to pull down...to build and to plant." (Cf. Jeremiah 1:10; 18:7–9; 45:4.) In the same tradition, see Hosea 6:1 on "tear—heal" and "strike—bind up," and perhaps more radically, Deuteronomy 32:39; Isaiah 45:7; and Job 5:18.

do not understand and to rely on that which they cannot control. It is the gift of breaking out of symmetrical language and symmetrical expectations into a context where hopes are actualized in surprising and even ragged ways.

There is little doubt that we live in a world of powerful, controlling people (read "kings"), where the voice of the prophet is scarcely heard or little honored, for notions of newness are unsettling at best and often disruptive. There is little doubt that the technical mind has triumphed, for now, in technical education, technical medicine, and all the rest. And poets are either kooks, or they are put on the payroll. Or they may even be kooks who are also on the payroll, but they are seldom permitted to speak their vision of a world bursting in on us.

Shalom affirms that in a world of kings, prophets must be heard and taken seriously; that in a world of technicians, the voice of the poet is essential for the humanness of our world. That is where the church might take its stand. We are in danger of silencing the prophets, domesticating the poets, and squeezing out the sources of newness among us. This danger implies an agenda for the church.

Obviously it is easier to state such an agenda than to bring it off. But that is the hard place where the crucifixion-resurrection people have always been called to be. It is the tension between those who dream about what is yet to be given in God's promises and those who manage what is already possessed. And surely that is what our best Reformation heritage is about: that we do not live by what is possessed but by what is promised. The possessed and the promised may for us be a useful way to talk about "works and faith," about (a) securing our own existence by prudent management of our resources and (b) receiving our existence as a gift freely given by the generous One. As Jürgen Moltmann has asserted, the really troublesome issue before us today is not the neat split of individual and corporate life, though some political ideologies would have it so. Nor is it body versus soul, though we have our alienations there also. Rather, it is the struggle among us and within us wherein we are defenders of the past and receivers of what is yet to come.

The two central conflicts of the Bible put it clearly. Pharaoh versus Moses is about the same issue. Pharaoh is the competent manager and desperate retainer of what has been and is. Moses is the terrifying voice of what is promised and surely will come in spite of the world's best resistances. Jesus versus the Pharisees of his time is the same. The Pharisees and all their allies in Jerusalem and Rome were those who had stabilized their lives and defended their turf powerfully. Then Jesus discounted and dismantled their prized situations. He announced that the promises were happening: The kingdom of God is at hand. The coming has come. The promises are being kept. And kings and technicians and pharaohs and Pharisees—all of us who have things stabilized—view newness as a most unwelcome guest. If we can, we shall uninvite this guest.

We live by what is promised and by what is yet to come. In that context I propose that we spend a little time reflecting on the great promises. Perchance we shall find in them reason to loosen our knuckle-whitening hold on what we possess. Just listen to these:

> He shall not judge by what his eyes see,
>   or decide by what his ears hear;
> but with righteousness he shall judge the poor,
>   and decide with equity for the meek of the earth...
>
> The wolf shall live with the lamb,
>   the leopard shall lie down with the kid,
> the calf and the lion and the fatling together,
>   and a little child shall lead them...
>
> They will not hurt or destroy
>   on all my holy mountain;
> for the earth will be full of the knowledge of the LORD
>   as the waters cover the sea. (Isaiah 11:3–4a, 6, 9)
>
> For I am about to create new heavens
>   and a new earth;
> the former things shall not be remembered
>   or come to mind...
> No more shall the sound of weeping be heard in it,
>   or the cry of distress.
> No more shall there be in it
>   an infant that lives but a few days,
>   or an old person who does not live out a lifetime...
> They shall build houses and inhabit them;
>   they shall plant vineyards and eat their fruit.

They shall not build and another inhabit;
    they shall not plant and another eat…
Before they call I will answer,
    while they are yet speaking I will hear.
The wolf and the lamb shall feed together,
    the lion shall eat straw like the ox…
They shall not hurt or destroy on all my holy mountain,
    says the LORD. (Isaiah 65:17, 19–22, 24–25)

on that day there will be a highway from Egypt to Assyria, and the Assyrian will come into Egypt, and the Egyptian into Assyria, and the Egyptians will worship with the Assyrians.

On that day Israel will be the third with Egypt and Assyria, a blessing in the midst of the earth, whom the LORD of hosts has blessed, saying, "Blessed be Egypt my people, and Assyria the work of my hands, and Israel my heritage." (Isaiah 19:23–25)

The days are surely coming, says the LORD, when I will make a new covenant with the house of Israel and the house of Judah. It will not be like the covenant that I made with their ancestors when I took them by the hand…I will be their God, and they shall be my people…I will forgive their iniquity, and remember their sin no more. (Jeremiah 31:31–34)

You, of course, know all these texts. Each one obviously could be pursued in detail because they are rich with powerful imagery. But my purpose in including them is to put all of them on you at one time. My purpose is not to have you grasp the details of the vision of any particular passage, but to have you caught up in and overwhelmed by the impact of the whole. Obviously something powerful and incredible is going on here, namely, the announcement of a world not yet known or possessed, but a world promised that will surely come. It is the doxology of a community fully freed and reconciled, in which every form of hurt and fear has been overcome. That is what is promised and what is to come. And that is the song of the promises and the image of the poets, the voices of Moses and of Jesus, that a new world is about to be given, and we can trust ourselves to it and live as though in it.

The forward thrust and the passionate, confident waiting are not reduced in New Testament passages. Most supremely Paul writes:

> For the creation waits with eager longing for the revealing of the children of God; for the creation was subjected to futility, not of its own will but by the will of the one who subjected it, in hope that the creation itself will be set free from its bondage to decay and will obtain the freedom of the glory of the children of God. We know that the whole creation has been groaning in labor pains until now; and not only the creation, but we ourselves, who have the first fruits of the Spirit, groan inwardly while we wait for adoption, the redemption of our bodies. (Romans 8:19–23)

Those are heavy expectations: "children of God," "freedom of the glory of the children of God," "adoption," all waiting for a time of full empowerment, acceptance, and belonging. That is what we trust in. It has been promised, and the One who promises is faithful. Moreover, we trust this faithful One! And we know about this One. We know from the exodus that this God has come out for freedom and justice against slavery and oppression. We know from the resurrection that God has come out for life against death. And so we wait, but we wait with confidence.

But we do more than wait. We are bold to say that in Jesus of Nazareth—before our very eyes—that for which we wait has begun to happen. The promises have begun to be fulfilled. The long-expected primordial king who is able to still the waters has begun to do it before our eyes, in our experience. Promises are for keeping, and he talked about it:

> "Ask, and it will be given you; search, and you will
>   find;
>   knock, and the door will be opened for you.
> For everyone who asks receives, and everyone who
>   searches finds, and for everyone who knocks, the
>   door will be opened…
> How much more will your Father in heaven give good
>   things to those who ask him!" (Matthew 7:7–8, 11)

How radical can you get! Jesus dared to assert that people who live expectantly, people who wait for promises, are the ones who are blessed. And it has begun, and we belong to a long history of those who have found it so.

But there is more radical affirmation than that. You know the remarkable conversation he had when the seventy disciples came to report to him:

(Disciples) "Lord, in your name even the demons submit to us!"

(Jesus) "I watched Satan fall from heaven like a flash of lightning. See, I have given you authority to tread on snakes and scorpions, and over all the power of the enemy; and nothing will hurt you." (Luke 10:17–19)

That is very strange talk. Can you think of a more radical claim than that, that he saw Satan fall from the sky? He saw the throne of evil toppled and the pretender fall off the platform. He is saying to his disciples: "You ain't seen nothing yet. There is more to come, and it's coming now." Jesus shares with his disciples the bold celebration that the world has been changed, and the way that it is now ordered is not the way it has been ordered, nor the way it seems to be ordered. It still seems to be a place of fear, resentment, and threat, a place of serpents and enemies. But they have all been defanged. They cannot hurt you. The power of hurt and hate, the force of death and destruction, has been overcome. He promised that, and there it is. The one who seems to be in charge is not in charge. Jesus promised that, and you can count on it. The holy One is in charge, and the dehumanizing power has no hold over us.

The world is too preoccupied with its petty, desperate attempts to secure its own existence. But there is good news. Even though you still sense all those threats and dangers, Satan has already been defeated. Our salvation is already guaranteed. God has already intervened, even though its fulfillment is yet to happen among us.

Our waiting for fulfilled promises is always causing us to affirm in two directions: It has happened; it is yet to happen. But we need not puzzle over that subtle riddle. It is enough for us to know that the world is being changed by the power of God for the purposes of God. The Lord has not reneged on this intention and, therefore, we are free to live other kinds of lives. We are free to deploy our energies in new ways and spend our funds and build our programs in new directions.

The turn in the world for which we have desperately and yearningly waited is upon us. And in our managing, royal, technical mind-set, we are tempted to miss it. But the voice of the prophet and the vision of the poet speak to us about the turn that God is doing according to God's word.

We order our lives differently because we know something the world doesn't know. We embrace a vision the world doesn't honor, and we trust a promise keeper that the world does not trust. Does it boggle your mind to receive a special invitation to live in the new age? Does it frighten you to think of leaving the old age, the old patterns of behavior, our accustomed loyalties, and our favorite fears and angers? *Shalom* is talk about new-age stuff. It is about new-age faith but also new-age politics. It is about new-age love but also new-age justice.

Gerhard von Rad[3] and Hans Walter Wolff[4] have shown us how to read the book of Genesis as a statement about old age/new age. The old age is presented in Genesis 3—11, a world filled with mistrust and greed, with fear and suspicion, with destruction and alienation. It is a world in which no significant words are exchanged between persons and no new vision is held out. And the new age is the story of our family in Genesis 12—50, of Abraham who walked by faith, who received an heir in his hopelessness, who risked his land for his nephew, and who pursued a land promised but unknown and unnamed to him. The old age is the way the world has been, and there is no joy there. The new age is one in which blessings are given and received. And the focus, as von Rad has shown so well, is that turn in Genesis 12 in which the world in Abraham is called to repent, that is, to cease to walk by calculating sight and to walk by faith, receiving a word Abraham could ponder, but not explain.

That old age/new age pattern in Genesis is how it is with Jesus as well. He called all sorts of victims of the old age to a new world. He

---

[3]Gerhard von Rad, *Old Testament Theology* 1 (New York: Harper and Brothers, 1962), 160–75, has shown that Genesis 12:1–3 is the hinge between saving history and world history, and that Genesis 12—50 presents a history of promise in contrast to the promiseless history of the old age in Genesis 1—11. See also von Rad, *Genesis* (Philadelphia: Westminster Press, 1961), 148–56; *Old Testament Theology* 1, 105–21; and especially *Old Testament Theology* 2 (London: Oliver and Boyd, 1965), 319–35, on von Rad's articulation of promissory history. On the broader significance of von Rad's work on the old age/new age theme, see M. Douglas Meeks, *Origins of the Theology of Hope* (Philadelphia: Fortress Press, 1974), chapter 2.

[4]Hans Walter Wolff, "The Kerygma of the Yahwist," *Interpretation* 20 (1966) contrasts the history of curse with the history of blessing in Genesis.

invited competent people of sight to walk by faith (cf. Mark 10:17–22; John 3:5–8). Those deprived in the old age he invited to share the blessings of the new age (Luke 19:1–10).

> You were taught to *put away* your former way of life, your old self...and to be renewed in the spirit of your minds, and *clothe yourselves* with the new self, created according to the likeness of God in true righteousness and holiness. (Ephesians 4:22–24)

Put off the old age and all its images and expectations and mind-sets and patterns of behavior. Put on the new age, new expectations, new identity, new ways of being and living. The old age/new age talk is radical and abrupt and sounds like tent revival talk, but churches like ours cannot abandon it to fundamentalist groups. It is our language and our tradition. It is the central biblical way of affirming that newness can come, that there can come death and new life to us, that the world can be radically changed and our way of being in the world can be transformed. But in our church tradition, we do not confine old age/new age talk to personal living, as do some others. The old age/new age issue also concerns public issues and institutional ordering in life. The new age is concerned not only with joy but also with justice, not only with love but also with equality, not only with happy persons but also with nurtured environment.

All of us at times like the way it was. And when we talk about the new, the world will indeed hate us. That is why the cross is the central symbol for *shalom,* our major identifying symbol, and why it is also the ugly embodiment of rejection and hostility. The cross in the life of Jesus and in the life of the church fully expresses old age/new age imagery.

- The cross is about abandonment of the old, in all its preciousness.
- The cross is about embrace of the new, in all its terror and precariousness.
- The cross is about repentance, of departing and entering.

We have so much to abandon:

- efforts to secure our existence
- efforts to control our brothers and sisters
- efforts to possess it all

We have so much to embrace:

- the gift of life and security freely given
- the generous care of brothers and sisters
- the joy of receiving the world God entrusts to us for our care

Next time (and I hope it's soon) that you are at the eucharistic table, notice how the old age/new age drama is played out in the elements. It consists in our giving up the elements, our surrendering them to God's rule and use. God takes them, and blesses and breaks them. They are given back to us, and we are invited to receive and embrace. Something dramatic has happened. What we bring to the table is our produce, even our property. But when handled by the Lord, it becomes a gift to us. The new age is to have our life handed back to us, after it is broken (God's rule established) and after it is blessed (empowered as gift). Our life handed back to us under God's rule and empowered is what the new age is about. The world hates that. It also rejects it, because with the mind of technical reason it thinks nothing has happened. It requires the hope of a prophet and the vitality of a poet to know that everything has happened. Life has been given up, and it has been received again. All things are new.

It behooves us to locate the spots in our existence where the new age has begun to happen, and where the old age lingers with power. We are called to abandon and to embrace. That's how it is with God and God's people.

12

SHALOM TOOLS

After he had washed their feet, had put on his robe, and had returned to the table, he said to them, "Do you know what I have done to you? You call me Teacher and Lord—and you are right, for that is what I am. So if I then, your Lord and Teacher, have washed your feet, you also ought to wash one another's feet. For I have set you an example, that you also should do as I have done to you. Very truly, I tell you, servants are not greater than their master, nor are messengers greater than the one who sent them. If you know these things, you are blessed if you do them. I am not speaking of all of you; I know whom I have chosen. But it is to fulfill the scripture, 'The one who ate my bread has lifted his heel against me.'"

JOHN 13:12–18

The current emphasis on *shalom* means to raise the question about the church: What does it mean to be the church in any case? But more particularly, what does it mean to be a church that is about the gift and task of *shalom?* How do we get it all together in the Christian community so that our life together expresses God's will for the way people are expected to live? Some preliminary observations:

1. *Any serious attempt at renewal in the church must be concerned with both structure and mood.* Many Protestant churches continue to be preoccupied with structure and have put a lot of effort into getting our decision making and program development procedures shaped up. Perhaps we have been insensitive to the mood in which we do our business. Theology isn't exactly popular in the church. But we also have a long history of caring and have assumed that if we cared enough, it would somehow work out. We have learned that such unplanned caring might result in the perpetuation of paternalistic inequality. So careful planning about structure is essential to protect us from the intentional or unintentional results of unplanned caring. The issue is, How do we create structures to match our caring?

2. Shalom *is a question that concerns every level and dimension of church life, local to national, from action to piety.* This is expressed in the call for national church structures to strengthen the local parish. But we are double-minded very often because we are inventive about changing, adjusting, and even manipulating the national church, awhile we intend business as usual at home. *Shalom* does indeed ask how the big programming and budgeting of the national and conference life of the church can do its work. But it calls with equal vigor for a look at home to ask how parishes face in fresh ways the way to God's future, which we characterize by the word *shalom.*

3. *The issue in the church's being God's whole people is power.* The phrase "whole people" means all the people, but it also means the various people integrated into some kind of trusting, working organism toward some shared objectives. That is, "the whole people" refers not only to inclusive fellowship, but also to convinced mission.

When the Bible talks of *shalom,* it talks of well-being for widows and orphans, who are the ones designated by society as weak and helpless. To be a widow or orphan is not to be one who grieves forever about a loss. Rather, it is a legal or sociological designation about one who, because of the loss of husband or father, has no representation in the decision making of the community. The "whole people" theme thus raises the question about how the unrepresented get a share of social leverage, how they get a voice in priorities. "The whole people" bent toward *shalom,* then, is the entire community committed to sharing power with the powerless ones. And that means we must ask who the powerless ones are and how we share the power. But for beginners, we may observe that characteristically we prefer to talk about *shalom* and lots of other things without mentioning power. People who have it do not care to have it discussed, because to discuss it is to expose it and perhaps also to lose some of it.

So our theme is whole people. We begin with the recognition that we can't really be whole people until all folks are empowered to share in the life of the community. Our theme then is whole people empowering others to share in the wholeness. Here I want to focus on the last words of Jesus to his church just before he was gone. He gave them *shalom* of another kind; perhaps what he said there was a clue about how we can be the whole church empowering others to share in the wholeness.

Tools of the Trade

In that strange series of events, *the towel and basin are symbols of* shalom. Or perhaps it is better to say they are agents of *shalom.* The towel and basin are not only symbols, though they are that and powerful ones; they are the means by which something is done. In this dramatic act, Jesus offers tools to his church. And you know what he said when they had the tools in hand:

"So if I, your Lord and Teacher, have washed your feet, you also ought to wash one another's feet." (John 13:14)

What a horror and what a marvel! He said, "Now you know how. You do it." Surely someone there must have observed that a towel did not fit his hands. But then our hands must change and grow and become more flexible. I think of the tools of my work. They are books and computer and, if necessary, telephone. They are manageable tools, mostly hardware. But a towel is not something I use on other people, at most only when the kids are going to bed. A towel is not firm and manageable. It is flexible to the point of being shapeless. It receives its shape not really from my hands, but from the feet around which it is wrapped for drying purposes. Jesus gave us tools that are shaped not in the heat of conviction, but in the delicate touch of those whom we would include in the beloved community. It occurred to me that it is important that I use a towel only when I put my kids to bed, never at the seminary, never with students and colleagues—only at home in the privacy of my home in those intimate relations where, if I may put it so, I am performing my servant function. Could it be a sign to us that he gave us tools that, for that time, were the tools of a slave, in our time the tools of a servant? They were not the tools of a master, now the tools of a competent manager. The managers who run the junior baseball practice on Saturday morning do not present themselves as towel-and-basin people. But they manage with vigor.

The tools of our trade! The tools define the trade. We can do only what our tools permit us to do. And if we have the tools of a slave, we can do only that kind of work. The towel and basin are slave tools. They do the work no master would do, that is, they make contact with the repulsive, abhorrent dimensions of our humanity. The towel and basin are servant tools. They do the work no reputable, competent manager would do, that is, they make contact with dimensions of our humanity that need personal caring attention.

The Nature of the Trade

The towel and basin are a hard demand for the church from the Lord Jesus. The only trade we can practice is the one for which we have tools, and the tools he gave on that occasion were slave tools. It must be that our task is to make contact with the repulsive, abhorrent dimension of our humanity, to make contact with dimensions of our humanity that need personal caring attention. Let us not romanticize the mandate. It is not an attractive one. So I have been asking: How do folks like me get to where we can do that? The hint of an answer I get is that these tasks are done by people who can get their minds off themselves to focus full attention on the subject of ministry, on the poor and needy of the world in all their poverty and need. We need to get our minds off ourselves so that we fully, without grudge and perhaps with willing joy, enter into the plight and identify with the humanity of those who cry out for such caring service.

But consider what a slave does in such a posture. The positioning of one's self in that way serves to *position the other as master.* Now, it is no small matter to set one's fellow in the place of a master, and the drama of that is even more telling if the one who is being *raised* to masterhood is precisely the one who has been lowered and excluded. Folks are lowered in society; the worthless and disregarded sink lower and lower in the estimate of the community until they sink in their own estimate. And folks who are unacceptable can be excluded so long, so vigorously that they come to perceive themselves as excluded and excommunicated. Ministry to them is after the manner of the ministry of Jesus, which has two characteristics:

1. The ones *lowered* by everybody should be *raised*. This incredible resurrection word is precisely the one used by Jesus in his address to that paralytic: "I say to you, stand up, take your mat and go to your home" (Mark 2:11). It was, significantly, a paralytic, one so lowered he could not move, who was raised and restored to his humanness. It is this incredible resurrection word that the church through the mouth of Peter spoke to the lame man: "'In the name of Jesus Christ of Nazareth, stand up and walk.' And he took him by the right hand and *raised* him up" (Acts 3:6–7).

2. The ones *excluded* by everybody should be *included*. That incredible salvation word is precisely the one used by Jesus in his address to Zacchaeus, who surely was excluded: "Today salvation has come to this house, because he too is a son of Abraham" (Luke 19:9). Jesus made Zacchaeus again a child of the promise from which he had been excluded. That incredible salvation word is precisely the one the church, in the person of Peter, learned to speak when he received his instruction that the Lord includes what we exclude: "'What God has made clean, you must not call profane'…'God has shown me that I should not call anyone profane or unclean'" (Acts 10:15, 28). This is towel-and-basin attitude by the slave-servant church in contact with those who have never known what it was like to be elevated (enthroned) or included. Clearly the only church that can practice such a ministry is the one so sure of its own identity that it can confidently be a servant. The only church that can practice such a ministry is one so sure of its security in the face of its Lord that it can take a role not defined by competence and achievement. Surely when Jesus gave us the tools of the trade, he was not giving us tools to do better the trade we have always been in. But in that dramatic action, he was radically redefining the trade we practice. We are called to image our "churching" differently in the national bureaucracy and at the local level. The church is called to repent of its habits of judging folks and to begin raising them instead. It is called to repent of its posture of exclusion and to include that which is scarcely acceptable to us. Not just anybody can take up that towel and basin. The only ones who can do that are ones who have had their lives empowered by the gospel, who have been freed enough to live their lives out of a very different system of values. Thus, the towel and basin drastically call into question our sense of identity. It won't do for a "business as usual" church to take towel and basin in hand, because we will have

tools without heart to match. So the towel is not only a statement about mission and ministry; it is a statement about identity. It calls the church to the same posture as the Crucified One, who knows that death for obedience is a source of power. Surely a hard saying for people like us!

The Church under Mandate

The death the church is called to die can be articulated in many ways. In this narrative it means to face the conviction that *we are under commandment.* We are a mandated people: "I give you a new commandment" and the Latin *novum mandatum* suggest it; we are people under a new mandate. That's not very American. If Philip Rieff in his *The Triumph of the Therapeutic*[1] is correct, the idea of being under any mandate from anybody is an awkward notion in modern context, and if liberation from every demand is the only way to maximize human potential, then this language will not reach us. But the church's primitive rhetoric is not about actualizing our own potential, because we have no potential on our own. We have gifts only in our relation to God. Our being is in being bound to God, and the pursuit of autonomy cannot be our way in the world. So we talk about law and order, but we don't mean it. We mean it only for the others, while we bask in our affluent autonomy.

It is shattering to face the claim. The new commandment is not for them. It is for us. The church with a new mandate is obviously not envisioned to be a big or a popular church, but a church under discipline, the rigorous expectation that we are open enough, have time enough, and care enough to take one another seriously. That is how we shall be the whole people, isn't it? And isn't that what it means to love one another? It does not mean to romanticize or to fawn over one another, but to take one another with deep seriousness. I find it hard to take some people seriously because they surely, by my lights, are wrong. It is shattering that I am mandated in the church to take them seriously. And we know now in the church that people who do not take one another seriously in their deep differences will never be a church with any kind of power. We are a church like every other group of folks, filled with persons who are hurting and waiting to be taken seriously, who are rejoicing and waiting to be taken seriously.

---

[1]Philip Rieff, *The Triumph of the Therapeutic* (New York: Harper and Row, 1966).

It is so obvious. But also demanding. The whole people must pay attention to its own life and its own folks. We know but forget certain basics about love:

- Love for the brother and the sister is what lets the church be, not morality or doctrine or piety.
- Love means to empower, to cause to be fully.
- Love is the central mark of the church.

This is what it means to take Jesus seriously as Lord. And, of course, we have forgotten that. We have made the mark of the church the right tag words of doctrine or of piety. Or we have preferred a certain social ideology of the left or of the right. But to love the brothers and sisters enough to raise and include them, that is a mandate of another dimension that comes to us with pain.

The "business as usual" church can't add that on to its life. So we have a "love one another" committee along with the others. No, this is the mainspring of life, and the only way to cut through the divisions that rip at us. The church is mandated not just to do kind things, but to perceive the world differently, to know that the wave of the future is not in putting people down, but in *raising them up;* the fruit of the kingdom is not in excluding but in *including.* In this action and this teaching, Jesus draws a sharp distinction between himself and the world's salvation systems, that is, the legal systems of competence and achievements. In his day and in ours, the way to security and well-being (read *shalom)* is by putting others down, which we call "getting ahead." And the circle of achievement depends on moving up to a place where the less competent are excluded. No wonder Jesus was such a threat, because he placed into question the world's way of ordering its life, doing its business, rewarding its adherents, and punishing its dissenters! And in like manner, Jesus draws a distinction between his church and all other communities of meaning and salvation. This community is both to order its own life differently and to posture itself toward the world differently.

A New Identity

The church invited to the work of raising up and including is called to change *its self-understanding and self-identity.*

"I do not call you servants any longer…but I have called you friends." (John 15:15)

The difference between servant and friend is clear and heavy. The servant does not know what the master is doing or intends. The servant doesn't ask questions, but dully does the assigned piece of unthinking work. But the friend is one who knows what the master does and cares what the master intends. To be a friend of the One who dies and is risen does not mean to be his buddy or his casual acquaintance, but to be his confidant, to share his intent, perhaps to be in on the planning, to invest in his dreams and his anxieties. Imagine that! Taken into God's dreams for the world, which the world itself rejects and fears. To be in on a secret that to know is to be a doomed person in the eyes of the world.

I don't know about you, but as for me, I would rather be a servant—go through the motions, finish the clearly defined day, and go home and not worry about it all. But this other relation is burdensome. It means to be there with him through it all.

Among other things, this is a warning against the church's spending its life on unreflective trivia. We get caught sometimes like a mindless slave, without a sense of proportion or focus or priority, but endlessly doing the task we started, like a secretary told to fold papers who never asks why or how many, but goes on and on in a meaningless way.

But the friends know the master's intent. They were present at the articulation of the costly vision of how it could be when persons are raised and included. Perhaps it is not far-fetched to see in this announcement of Jesus to his friends a remote allusion to the old office of "king's friend" (see 2 Samuel 15:37; 16:16), which was apparently a high office in the old royal apparatus.[2] The reference there is apparently to a specific office of great prestige and influence with the king—that is, his special confidant—and close to the throne. If that connection can even be suggested, the church is offered here a place in the councils of the Lord where the decisions are made, but also where the payroll must be met and the rent paid. Although it is a position of assurance, it may require the costly rent he alluded to in

---

[2]See the summary statement of Roland de Vaux, *Ancient Israel* (New York: McGraw-Hill, 1961), 122–23. In a more specific study, A. van Selms, "The Origins of the Title 'The King's Friend,'" *Journal of Near Eastern Studies* 16 (1957): 118–23, suggests the title originally referred to the king's best man at his wedding, who subsequently became his intimate royal confidant. Certainly I do not suggest such a meaning in the Fourth Gospel, but the special role, intimacy, and confidentiality of the formula in the Fourth Gospel is not dissimilar to the nuances of the older title.

Mark 10:35–45, the rent of the baptism and cup of the cross. We have privy information about God's intent for the world, and since then, we are marked men and women bearing a secret vision the world cannot tolerate. But isn't it great to know it and to be invited to live it!

Strength for the Task

It is no wonder that this church was the one promised the Spirit. If you put all this together, it is a church sitting on a powder keg where God's explosion might happen. Here it is with

1. the tools of the trade, which call us to raise up and include others
2. a new mandate to reform our lives
3. a new understanding and identity as the officers of the king, privy to his royal visions and dreams

The whole people is the one that has faced the vocation "No more business as usual." The church is called to be who it has not been and to do what it has never thought of doing. The church is called to be engaged in the unthinkable.

We are, of course, not sure if that is possible. Most of the church as we experience it consists of reviewing last year's budgets and plans and doing them again, or at best reshuffling the pieces. But now the unthinkable. We are mostly people heavily committed to the thinkable and the manageable and the measurable. For folks such as us to take the tools, the mandate, and the identity offered at the table will take a great gust of God's breath, and that's what is promised to us. The coming of the Spirit, the counselor that has been promised, is that which might bring us to the unthinkable. And the unthinkable, no matter where it meets us, is shaped like a cross that has been known and emptied in triumph. The unthinkable is among the wretched who are becoming the beloved. The unthinkable is the facing of death, perhaps institutional death, and knowing that therein is the gift of life.

The church is not, and perhaps never will be, ready for such unthinkability. But on the night of arrest and betrayal, the day before execution as an enemy of the state, normally thinkable thoughts hardly are worth thinking. Think about it!

13

THE *SHALOM* CHURCH

When he had gone out, Jesus said, "Now the Son of Man has been glorified, and God has been glorified in him. If God has been glorified in him, God will also glorify him in himself and will glorify him at once. Little children, I am with you only a little longer. You will look for me; and as I said to the Jews so now I say to you, 'Where I am going, you cannot come.' I give you a new commandment, that you love one another. Just as I have loved you, you also should love one another. By this everyone will know that you are my disciples, if you have love for one another."

Simon Peter said to him, "Lord, where are you going?" Jesus answered, "Where I am going, you cannot follow me now; but you will follow afterward." Peter said to him, "Lord, why can I not follow you now? I will lay down my life for you." Jesus answered, "Will you lay down your life for me? Very truly, I tell you, before the cock crows, you will have denied me three times.

"Do not let your hearts be troubled. Believe in God, believe also in me. In my Father's house there are many dwelling places. If it were not so, would I have told you that I go to prepare a place for you? And if I go and prepare a place for you, I will come again and

*will take you to myself, so that where I am, there you may be also.
And you know the way to the place where I am going."*

JOHN 13:31—14:4

*"I am the true vine, and my Father is the vinegrower. He removes
every branch in me that bears no fruit. Every branch that bears
fruit he prunes to make it bear more fruit. You have already been
cleansed by the word that I have spoken to you. Abide in me as I
abide in you. Just as the branch cannot bear fruit by itself unless it
abides in the vine, neither can you unless you abide in me. I am the
vine, you are the branches. Those who abide in me and I in them
bear much fruit, because apart from me you can do nothing. Whoever
does not abide in me is thrown away like a branch and withers;
such branches are gathered, thrown into the fire, and burned. If
you abide in me, and my words abide in you, ask for whatever you
wish, and it will be done for you. My Father is glorified by this,
that you bear much fruit and become my disciples."*

JOHN 15:1–8

*"If the world hates you, be aware that it hated me before it hated
you. If you belonged to the world, the world would love you as its
own. Because you do not belong to the world, but I have chosen you
out of the world—therefore the world hates you. Remember the
word that I said to you, 'Servants are not greater than their master.'
If they persecuted me, they will persecute you; if they kept my word,
they will keep yours also."*

JOHN 15:18–20

I want to reflect on the *shalom* motifs in John 13 and following,
which have been called the Farewell Addresses of Jesus. I have settled
here for two reasons. First, Frederick Herzog's book *Liberation Theology*
has presented a most suggestive exegesis, and I want to relate to that.[1]
My own suggestions are quite independent of his, but I have learned
much from him. Second, and more important, I have wanted to locate
a time in the church (albeit in the early church) that is like our own,

---

[1]Frederick Herzog, *Liberation Theology* (New York: Seabury Press, 1972).

when the church experienced what we experience, namely, our Lord's bewildering absence (or is it hidden presence?), which leaves us nearly directionless. So I thought such a time might be when he said goodbye to his disciples and left them alone, surely confused and perhaps waiting. And perchance that farewell in the Fourth Gospel still holds, and we are still left without him, surely confused and perhaps waiting. And when he leaves, we are there alone to manage our faith and ministry, to live only with the memory of his parting words, the conviction that he comes again, and the in-betweenness of his assuring words about a comforter. Of these, what we have most surely here are his parting words. Those are preserved for us in this curious tradition. Whatever critical judgments may be made about this text—and the scholars do not agree—these words were framed and valued and transmitted as such in the church.

My purpose is to remind us of what Jesus said as he left us, and to invite us all to reflect on it. Related to *shalom*, the words that I consider central are these:

> "*Peace* I leave with you; my *peace* I give to you. I do not give
> to you as the world gives. Do not let your hearts be troubled,
> and do not let them be afraid." (John 14:27)

That's all he said. And then he left. And the rest of our history as his receiving church has been wondering what he meant when he said that. That is a very strange departure, and I want to share these observations about those strange words, which perhaps are the most haunting and possibly the most decisive for our self-understanding.

1. These words—all these speeches—are spoken to the church in the context of the Lord's supper. It is at the table that we have always found his reassuring presence.

(a) At the table we eat and drink to another reality and toward another order. I grow more convinced that if we are to understand *shalom* at all, we shall understand it at the table. It is at the table as nowhere else that we get our minds off ourselves long enough to think of God's promises and God's tasks. Most of the time the church is busy worrying about well-being, survival, reputation, success. At the table, we occasionally put those temptations in perspective and see that they do not really matter. No doubt it is not possible for us as the church, any more than any other community, to live always with that demanding, reassuring awareness. But what a marvel and a gift! We have given to us and can value that moment of truth when we come face-to-face with realities that let us break free of our immobilizing self-preoccupation.

(b) At the table as nowhere else we are made aware that true life is in mystery and not in management. At the table there is no worry about numbers of members or budget, but only the reminder of meanings given that we don't have to explain or manufacture. It is overpowering, when we reflect on it, that all the key verbs in that drama have him as subject and not us. We are the subject of no important active verbs at the table. He took and he blessed and he broke and he gave to us again. It is his table; we are welcome guests, and we don't fix the menu or pay the bill.

(c) It follows that at the table, as nowhere else, we are the Lord's, not ours. We are not ours, and he is not ours. We need not worry there about our destiny. We do not have to justify our existence there. I find that freedom and gift nowhere else completely. Probably we have not been enough amazed at that incredible gift God has granted us in the mystery of the table. There we need only yield our lives to God. That is all. As such, the table stands in contrast to, if not in protest against, all the ways we think we have to make it the rest of the time. Do not miss the polemical point I am suggesting by starting our discussion of *shalom* at the table. I have the impression that most of us, and perhaps we cannot do otherwise, want to talk about *shalom* as task, or as discipleship, or (perish the thought) as "works," as more we have to do. If we start there, we not only betray the mystery of the table but also doom our *shalom-ing* to failure, either in pride or despair, before we even begin.

But it does begin at the table. It always does. And the promise to us is that the church that lets this historic mystery fashion its life can hear the word and can be empowered to live in and toward the new age of *shalom*.

2. The church that has been to the table and has heard the word has nothing to fear:

Do not let not your hearts be troubled, and do not let them be afraid.

In these days, fear is deep and broad in the land and in the church. Fear does strange things to people. It makes us withdraw from our brothers and sisters and live in a crouch. It makes us attracted to a fetal position. It makes us say things and do things that do not honor us. It makes us hurt one another—all because we fear the world is falling apart. Fear is our modern form of atheism, fear that there is no order but the one I invent. Thus, I must protect what little order I have, scramble to make more, and keep people from intruding on my order or my mystery or my goodies, because if they come there, it will all fall apart. There is no one but me, and I must hustle. Jesus is surely right on target when he asks his church, "Why are you afraid? Have you still no faith?" (Mark 4:40). Fear is lack of confidence that Jesus' order and his promises will endure his departure. Are we not like the little baby so popularized by Erik Erikson,[2] who cries because he fears his mother will not return? So fear, atheism, is linked to our primal sense of abandonment. Surely the church was frightened that day because Jesus was leaving, and then all the risks and promises and uncertainties were exposed.

But here it is! This is what he said: "Do not fear!"[3] It's the same primal word that the angels of God have always spoken to men and women of faith when called to be bold in action and affirmation (Genesis 15:1; Isaiah 41:10, 13–14; 43:1; 44:8; Jeremiah 1:8; 30:10–11; Matthew 28:5; Luke 1:30; 2:10). The world is God's, and it will not fall apart. The new age that the Lord has begun cannot be driven out or held back. The church need not live out of fear as though the gospel were not true. It is destined to live toward freedom, toward the pain of the world, toward the hurt of the world, toward the joy of the world—the pain and hurt that the world does not understand and the joy that the world does not anticipate. As he left he reminded the church that we are able to risk much because we are safe. We may need to focus much on *shalom* as a task, but it begins at the table as assurance. It is pure gift, and it is delivered in the rhetoric that has been most authoritative among our people.

3. Then he lays on us some more meaning from the table. In his statement about who we shall be and how we shall order the faith and

---

[2]Erik Erikson, *Childhood and Society* (New York: W. W. Norton and Company, 1963), 247–51.
[3]Cf. Walter Brueggemann, *Cadences of Home: Preaching among Exiles* (Louisville, Ky.: Westminster John Knox Press, 1997), 48–49.

ministry entrusted to us, he tells us who we are, a precious image out of our past: "You are branches." Very quickly, two things are clear about branches. One, they stay close to the vine. And you know who the vine is, the one who just left, so stay close to the absent one. In our kind of church, we do not reflect often enough on what it means to stay close to Jesus, to be connected to him, especially in his absence. This is not to propose some new moralism or some new pietism. But we do not need to be so sophisticated and secular that we must keep a distance from him as Peter did at the trial. So we may live by the joy of Jesus, who rejoiced at upsetting newness. We may live by the risk of Jesus, who emptied himself. We may live by the power of Jesus, which other folks thought to be weakness. He always surprised them by drawing power from perceived weakness. We may live by the dreams of Jesus, which are not unlike the dreams of Martin Luther King, Jr.—eloquent fantasies about a new age surely to surge among us. All of that—joy, risk, power, and dreams—all of that was about a new age being born among us; we dare not and need not settle in, either grimly or complacently, on the old age, which is passing away. Of course, that is nonsense, and the world knows that—the world that crucified Jesus, the older brothers who sent the dreamer Joseph off to slavery—because the world cannot abide such dreams. False dreams are so scary. We are invited to stay close to Jesus and draw on the sources of ministry and resilience that he used. We are invited to stay with the bold one, to take care not to get sucked in by any of the timid ones. Until I reflected on it, I thought the imagery of vine-branches was stale if not static. But it is a radical business, inviting us to stay connected to God and therefore not to be connected elsewhere. And if we belong to the grape family, our business is grapes—perhaps the wine of the new kingdom—and we are not permitted to produce briers or even eggplant or okra, but only the wine of the new age.

Producing is the second thing a good vine does: it bears fruit. It is from the vine that we receive life and identity so we can produce fruit appropriate to the vine, that is, if we stay connected to the vine. So we bear fruit like the fruit of the vine, and you know how that stuff looks and tastes. The fruit of Jesus is justice and freedom, love and hope, and everywhere he went, the soil of human intention produced fruit it never knew about before. Now that is heady stuff. Imagine, a little band of disciples on the day of his arrest, and he says this incredible, cosmic thing to them: "You are the ones." You are the ones to bear

fruit befitting my own personal intervention. That's not like the fruit
I think appropriate to me, which is characterized as security, well-
being, success, complacency. The little band in Jerusalem is not called
to bear its own favorite produce, but the stuff that comes from the
vine. It's still the same between church and Lord, between branch
and vine, and he says in effect to a little bunch of Christians in Webster
Groves or in Lancaster or in Peoria: "You are the ones to bear fruit
that resembles the vine." And you know the harvest: freedom such as
he gave, hope such as he offered, justice such as he promised, wholeness
such as he envisioned. What is going on is the creation of a whole
orchard of *shalom.*

4. This process of productivity surely is not letting the world
determine the agenda. It is letting the vine determine the harvest.
And, of course, the world has always been opposed to his kind of
fruit. The world resists freedom and hope and justice and wholeness.
The disciples knew it at that table that night. The world is hostile to
Jesus' kind of *shalom.* The world—and that means us and folks like
us—is committed to slavery, to despair, to oppression, and to
fragmentation. So he offers the kind of fruit the world isn't buying,
and he invites us to be the same kind of branches, and, sure enough,
it will get for us what it got for him.

You can see it as he walks out the door and they are still stunned
with his assertion: "The world will hate you." There surely ensued an
argument: "What will they say if we try to do that?" And Jesus almost
flippantly says, "Oh well, they hated me before they hated you. Pay
no attention to it." Imagine, his farewell speech, and just as he walks
out the door he casually observes, "Oh, by the way, they won't like
it." The Fourth Gospel has not very subtly announced one bold posture
on the Christ-culture issue. The world will hate you. The encounter
at the table has evolved so that now something else is going on here.
No longer do we have the assurance of the eucharist. Now we have
the rejection of the world. It is easy to be for *shalom* at the table, even
his hard kind of *shalom.* But now it's *shalom* in the world.

And in our kind of culture-accommodating religion in middle
America, that is sticky. It's so hard for us in America—or wherever
the church is called to testing—so hard to realize that our notions of
shalom are not going to be popular with the world. We stand for
commitments and values and dreams that the world hates and fears.
You know the list: crime, war, pollution, discrimination, education,

housing, employment. We are not called to please the world. It's easy for me to say, "Risk it," and then take the next plane home. But it's not my word. The parting shot of Jesus himself says, "Bear fruit that you know the world will not like."

The struggle going on at that table that night did not have to do with mounting a program for social action. It was no big deal social action program from a band of wanted men in hostile Jerusalem. Rather, the issue was having enough identity to survive. So the issue at the table, like the issue is always at the table, is to be clear on who we are and how we are called to position ourselves vis-à-vis the world. It is so for the church today. The issue is not merely to mount social action, for that runs its brief course, and the world is resilient. Instead, it is to be clear on how we order our lives and our budgets and all our programs with our agenda of fruit that the world cannot tolerate. I have been helped by Max Stackhouse's book on *Ethics and the Urban Ethos.*[4] He asserts that our job is to discern and bring to visibility the credo of the social engineers and planners who make the broad urban issues that fix our destinies. Our primary business is not to chip away at little "causes," but to address the basic symbolic issues of what we believe, of what we trust and fear, of what we wish to enhance, and of what we wish to curtail, which are, of course, all God-questions. Surely it is obvious that we cannot call into question the symbolic depth of the urban ethos and the urban credo until we have made clear our own, that we are in the world to produce fruit the world will hate. The symbolic issues are hazardous and crucial in our time, and ours is a very weak and problematic symbol. Can the identity we derive from the table provide a basis for confrontation in the world? That's a hard question for them in Jerusalem and for us now in America.

The *shalom* from the table means to embody a kind of wholeness and freedom and justice that the world does not recognize or even know exists. It is to value and bear witness to precisely what the world fears most. There is something radical and revolutionary about the

---

[4]Max Stackhouse, *Ethics and the Urban Ethos* (Boston: Beacon Press, 1972). At the center of his study is the insistence that "Every ostensible natural model is rooted in a non-natural *credo,* is informed by the relativities of culture, and requires a humanly planned and designed effort to attain it. Every naturalist effort requires the construction, artificially, of doctrines and institutions to sustain their convictions and to establish new controls over human efforts...The question is not then...a question of nature, but...a question of credo and control, and the way in which credo and patterns of domination—political as well as technological—interact" (45).

charge of "peace" that Jesus leaves his church. He announces clearly
that his people are not like the world. You know some of the
manifestations of those differences:

- valuing persons over property
- valuing public concern over private interest
- valuing equality over elitism
- valuing well-being over productivity
- valuing human dignity over competence
- seeking power for the oppressed
- seeking right-mindedness for the fragmented.

You can continue the list. All of that is surely what Jesus was
concerned about. And if the vine, then the branches.

5. Jesus manages to keep his little flock off balance. He tosses out
these ideas and then moves along. Then he says, "I have said all this to
keep you from stumbling" (John 16:1). I don't know about you, but
I have the suspicion that it wouldn't be so bad to stumble a little bit
and not be the church so vigorously. Interesting, isn't it, that
theologians like to talk about the "fall of man," to use that kind of
classical male imagery; but here the concern is not the "fall of man,"
but the fall of the church. To fall away not from high standards, but
from precious identity. That is what we are always deciding in the
church. It is always the question of how much of Jesus' kind of *shalom*
we can bear. His *shalom* is very reassuring, but it is as costly as it is
reassuring. And when the issues are set, how much we would now
rather yield! How much easier to give in, to settle for the way of the
world! How much easier not to be so intensely the church, not to care
so much for the things of God; how much easier to let the world have
its way! The insidiousness, of course, is that the issues around which
we fall away are seldom big, dramatic deals. They come only a little at
a time, and we have done it, and we don't know we have done it until
it's too late. Or more likely, we are never aware we have done it.

But we are Jesus' people. We have eaten at his table. We have
heard his word. We are identified as the odd ones in the world, called
to be at odds with the world, ordained to call into question the world's
way of doing business. We are the ones who are not to fall away. In
most congregations, we have not many wise, not many rich, not many
powerful, not many of noble birth. But we are not called to transform
the world even if we work at it. We are called just not to fall away.

And we have been prayed for. Think of that. We have been prayed for by the Son to the Father, to the one who is able to keep us from stumbling. That may be the only distinguishing characteristic we have. We have been prayed for, and the prayer is that we not fall away.

6. Then he spoke of what was perhaps the most surprising thing to them—the coming of the Spirit. It is not easy for us in our kind of church to cut through the doctrinal stuff to get at the power of the affirmation. The Spirit comes to guide the church and to empower the church. It is, first of all, an odd notion—odd then, more odd now in a world nearly reduced to rationality—that power emerges among us. We are enabled to do things and are led to know what to do. It won't help us much to intellectualize about that. But we have this remarkable assurance from our departing Lord, and we have our historical memory to back it up. The evidence requires this conclusion: When the church has been fully the church, when we have run God's kind of risks and borne God's kind of fruit, power has come and guidance has been at hand. That perhaps is the supreme test of our faith in the world at the table.

The coming of the Spirit requires those two incredible acts of faith. First, it requires that we yield to a power not our own, which is to concede that we are not in charge and that we are not managers of our destiny and our ministry. *Shalom* is precisely the capacity to yield to the gift of power, which comes unexpectedly and unexplained and, therefore, is neither understood nor managed by us. But capacity to receive and yield is not what we nurture or value. We stress rather consistently control, mastery, and competence. And the more we master, control, and manage, the less we can yield to the gift. So the Spirit does not come among us. The table is for those ready to receive. It is our place of receptivity, and perhaps even rational liberals like us can yield to the power.

Second, the coming of the Spirit requires that we be open to guidance, to think thoughts and embrace values and take actions that we never thought we would do. For most of us the guidance to which we are open is at best prudential and calculating. But this is invitation to blind risk, which causes outlandish acts of caring. I can think of two rather dramatic examples. One, the foolishness of the United Church General Synod in St. Louis in 1973, taking time and spending enormous amounts of money to fly to California for a one-day gesture of support for the United Farm Workers. By all prudent standards it was foolishness, hardly expected to produce any results; but perhaps it was the breaking in of Christ's spirit both in St. Louis and in California. Second, the mockery of Martin Luther King, Jr.'s being shot in Memphis where he had gone on behalf of a garbage workers' strike. Of all places to die, one would hardly pick Memphis, and for a cause, hardly a garbage workers' strike. But there King went, widely perceived as a man under guidance. So who wants or needs that kind of guidance, the kind that penetrates our best judgments and cuts through all of that in scandalous ways to bring us to what the world calls foolishness? The word *scandal* is a precious one because the central scandal of our faith is that Jesus emptied himself and did the foolish thing on behalf of those nobodies the world had long ago dismissed. The scandal of the cross is precisely to bear fruits consistent with the vine, fruits the world will hardly bid on. That is the openness of this Spirit that has always guided receptive people to foolish actions. It is sheer foolishness to eat with publicans and tax collectors. It is indefensible nonsense to touch lepers, to dance with the dead and bring them to life. But that is what he did and why he got killed, and it is the work he left us to do.

One can hardly talk about the coming Spirit without commenting on the current rash of charisma among the churches. I am already predisposed to discount it as foolishness of a nongospel kind, and we must take care not to do that. But we can be sober enough about it to say that where the Spirit is, the one our Lord has promised, it is to empower people toward boldness and guide them to foolishness. And that permits us to sort out some things. The coming of Christ's spirit, the one to keep us from stumbling, is not a warm feeling or simply acts of irrationality; but it is characteristically *empowerment* to restore and heal and *guidance* to risk for the unvalued of the world whom God has not ceased to value. The Spirit empowers and guides this community to fruits befitting the vine to whom they are connected.

Now I do not make these remarks flippantly. I find this word from the departing Lord heavy and harsh. I am a well-cast academic who believes in quality control and standards and, above all, order. I have been asking how folks such as me can be empowered to boldness and guided to foolishness, recognizing as I ask that foolishness and power somehow go together. To me, that is an abhorrent combination. Think of that as the starting place of it all, that the empowered ones are *empowered to foolishness*. My natural reaction to that is that if foolishness is the condition of power, I would rather have my regular powerlessness with competence. But what a choice! I suppose the capacity to receive and to yield has to do with my identity, my self-concept, the way I know myself to be situated in the world.

This story suggests to me that the essential ingredients of a yielding, receiving identity are mediated in towel and basin. The disciples, of course, were aghast—with a horror and a marvel and a long silence in the room that night. Are you like me, with a long list of folks whose feet you would refuse to wash? I know, of course, what we have done conventionally with towel and basin. We have made them symbols for self-effacement, self-abasement, and humility. But it is possible to take it another way. Think what you do when you wash the feet of another:

- You kneel before them.
- You place yourself at their disposal.
- You come to them without defense, vulnerable, risking all, letting your life be lived in the land of another.

I suggest that the issue is not humility. It is vulnerability. I do not mean the pseudovulnerability of some "growth groups," where we bare all to get stroked a bit more. I mean that in a church such as ours, characterized by fear and mistrust and filled with greedy, ambitious persons (just like the world), we should place ourselves at the disposal of one another. To kneel in the presence of another is to be totally vulnerable, because you are in an excellent posture to have your face or your groin kicked in. Just one swift motion by your client, and there you are. I for one resist ever putting myself in that position, but our Lord has made himself vulnerable precisely in that way.

We are very slow to learn what we know. Kneeling before another in vulnerability empowers him or her. In bringing one's self to the posture of a servant, one bestows on the other mastery. Jesus came to the frightened failures who had abandoned their dreams (perhaps as we have) or to anxious successes who had nightmares about protecting their dreams (maybe as we have), and he knelt before them. His kneeling said this: "You are master. I make you master by being your servant. I value you. I take you seriously. I empower you." The secret of the cross is revealed to us at that table in the middle of the night: Being vulnerable empowers the other one.

Jesus enacted the crucifixion that night. That is what we mean in the oldest confession, "Christ died for my sins." We can say it: "Christ's vulnerability empowered us to life." Jesus' capacity to kneel that night in an empowering way surely stemmed from his identity, and we should not miss the point in the text. He is not a random man who just grabbed a towel. The act of the towel derived faithfully from who he knew himself to be:

> Jesus, knowing that the Father had given all things into his hands, and that he had come from God and was going to God, got up from the table, took off his outer robe, and tied a towel around himself. (John 13:3–4)

Jesus had identity questions, destiny issues, settled in his life. He knew that he was totally empowered by God; all things were given into his hand. And because that issue was settled, he was able to remove the garments, the outward signs of respect and control that the world acknowledges.[5] He was able to take all that off precisely because the real issues were elsewhere and were already settled. The issue was settled with God and, therefore, Jesus could act differently toward his brothers and his sisters. He knelt, not in humility or in fear, but in strength and confidence, prepared to have his face kicked in. His kneeling in empowering vulnerability is not an action of servility, but of the new shape of bold majesty. He is not in a servant position, but in a lordly posture, motivated by confidence because the identity questions were settled. It is a stance informed by security and self-respect and self-confidence, not resentment and anxiety. We already know in our own lives and church what happens when kneeling is informed by resentment. It burns itself out and yields nothing, and the last state is worse than the first. The vocation Jesus gives us is not simply towel and basin, but towel and basin with all the self-issues resolved.

The *shalom* church is not one where all the questions are open and unsettled. The church cannot forever live with anxiety about its own identity. It must make up its mind, and when it makes up its

---

[5]On the significance of garments and the risk in removal, see the study of Leonard Bickman, "Social Roles and Uniforms: Clothes Make the Person," *Psychology Today* (April, 1974): 49–51. The power of clothes is enormous. Of course, that is not a new insight, as exile-nakedness was regarded in the Bible as supreme humiliation and deprivation of power (e.g., Isaiah 47:2–3). Not surprisingly, Jesus "disclosed" his power at the table by removing his garments.

mind, it can be yielding and receiving and vulnerable. The same resolution opens us to the Spirit and brings us to the feet of brothers and sisters. Until those issues are settled, we are neither empowered and guided by the Spirit nor authentically vulnerable before the others. But the church that night caught a vision of a vulnerable, empowering ministry. What a church! Here is a whole ecclesiology for parishes such as the one where I belong. The church

- has no fear
- is a fruitful branch
- receives the hatred of the world
- resists falling away
- receives the Spirit toward foolishness
- makes itself vulnerable

All are marks of the man on the cross, precisely the vulnerability of the cross. The one in whom there is agony but no guile, the one who empowers people to personhood. For such a church, as for such a lord, identity is not in doubt. Security is not debatable. Destiny is not up for grabs. There is no ultimate anxiety. That church knows itself to be safe, loved, valued, taken seriously, a church for which a place has been prepared. Peter Berger et al. describe the price of modernity in which such issues for modern persons are never settled.[6] The folks that night at the table ended their homelessness. All the issues were settled; like their Lord, they knew where they had come from and where they were going. Such a church says with confidence, "Free at last, free at last, thank God Almighty, we are free at last!" And that is what we celebrate every time we go to the table. We do not celebrate our success or fidelity, our good feeling, or a "worship experience." We celebrate that the identity questions are settled, that anxiety is gone and therefore we are freed to regal vulnerability, to assume the posture of a king as Jesus did, a posture of empowerment for nobodies. The narrative of these addresses moves neatly from 13:3, where the issues are settled for Jesus, to 15:14–15, where the issues are settled for the church by being incorporated into Christ's certitude:

---

[6]Peter L. Berger, Brigitte Berger, and Hansfried Kellner, *The Homeless Mind: Modernization and Consciousness* (New York: Random House, 1973). Berger et al. make it clear that restlessness and a sense of displacement and anxiety are not an aberration in modern society, but an essential ingredient in the function of modern life.

"You are my friends if you do what I command you. I do not call you servants any longer, because the servant does not know what the master is doing; but I have called you friends, because I have made known to you everything that I have heard from my Father." (John 15:14–15)

God's secrets have been shared with us, and they concern us. They tell us who we are and what we are therefore freed to do.

It all happened at this table where the drama of power and vulnerability was played out. Most of our tables are lifeless and without power because they exclude. They lack every claim of vulnerability. This table yields life precisely because there are no conditions for coming. At this table we have to do with him, with the ultimately vulnerable one.

He left then. He left us that way—kneeling, hated, and vulnerable. But he also left us free and not in doubt. Free and not in doubt because he had spoken that person-giving, identity-settling word *shalom*. He said, "My *shalom* I give to you. I do not give to you as the world gives." That's all he said, and then he left. And we are left to make decisions about our faith and ministry. But what he said permits different decisions.

PART FIVE

Shalom Persons

14

THE *SHALOM* PERSON

After a long time the king of Egypt died. The Israelites groaned under their slavery, and cried out. Out of the slavery their cry for help rose up to God. God heard their groaning, and God remembered his covenant with Abraham, Isaac, and Jacob. God looked upon the Israelites, and God took notice of them.

EXODUS 2:23–25

They came to the other side of the sea, to the country of the Gerasenes. And when he had stepped out of the boat, immediately a man out of the tombs with an unclean spirit met him. He lived among the tombs; and no one could restrain him any more, even with a chain; for he had often been restrained with shackles and chains, but the chains he wrenched apart, and the shackles he broke in pieces; and no one had the strength to subdue him. Night and day among the tombs and on the mountains he was always howling and bruising himself with stones. When he saw Jesus from a distance, he ran and bowed down before him; and he shouted at the top of his voice, "What have you to do with me, Jesus, Son of the Most High God? I adjure you by God, do not torment me." For he had said to him, "Come out of the man, you unclean spirit!" Then Jesus asked him,

"What is your name?" He replied, "My name is Legion; for we are many." He begged him earnestly not to send them out of the country. Now there on the hillside a great herd of swine was feeding; and the unclean spirits begged him, "Send us into the swine; let us enter them." So he gave them permission. And the unclean spirits came out and entered the swine; and the herd, numbering about two thousand, rushed down the steep bank into the sea, and were drowned in the sea.

The swineherds ran off and told it in the city and in the country. Then people came to see what it was that had happened. They came to Jesus and saw the demoniac sitting there, clothed and in his right mind, the very man who had had the legion; and they were afraid. Those who had seen what had happened to the demoniac and to the swine reported it. Then they began to beg Jesus to leave their neighborhood. As he was getting into the boat, the man who had been possessed by demons begged him that he might be with him. But Jesus refused, and said to him, "Go home to your friends, and tell them how much the Lord has done for you, and what mercy he has shown you." And he went away and began to proclaim in the Decapolis how much Jesus had done for him; and everyone was amazed.

MARK 5:1–20

All of us, implicitly or explicitly, have a doctrine of personhood. We believe something about persons that is likely to be a generalization of what we have come to believe about our own person. Here I want to see if the *shalom* motifs of scripture may present a different understanding of personhood.

Talking about *shalom* requires us to speak in terms of exodus and resurrection. So here, quite simply, a *shalom* understanding of personhood may be put another way: What do our memories of and convictions about exodus and resurrection tell us about personhood? I begin with the affirmation that these events are decisive for our self-understanding. And if they are decisive, surely they permit and require confessions about ourselves and preclude other notions of ourselves that would be neither permitted and required nor precluded apart from these events. These kinds of affirmations seem both possible and important out of those events.

Exodus

Exodus is, first of all, the story of persons appearing as active participants in history. We have already been through the whole secularization issue in popular theology, and we do not need to repeat it here. But we should not miss the radicalness of the beginning point of history for the people of Israel. Before this event they were not persons in history. They were slaves in Pharaoh's Egypt. They had no presence or identity. They were simply nameless slaves under bondage to quotas. Not only were they oppressed, but they settled for oppression as a way of life. Israel's history, and perhaps, we may claim, the history of humanity, begins the day the Israelites cry out.

> The Israelites groaned under their slavery, and cried out. Out of the slavery their cry for help rose up to God. (Exodus 2:23)

Human history, certainly Israelite history, begins in a *cry for freedom addressed in confidence that there is one who hears.* To cry for freedom is the assertion of personhood in the face of an ontological system that would deny our personhood. The brickyard of Pharaoh would just as soon keep everybody nameless slaves without identity, without confidence to cry out, without the terrifying confidence that there is one who hears. The cry of Israel in the brickyard is the protoannouncement in human history that personhood is possible, that it is willed, that it will be. And no oppressive system or presence can contain or silence that cry. Personhood as a theoretical notion, then, begins in the urging—the powerful urging—toward freedom. It appears in the brickyard as a *cry of rage* against the slavemaster but also as a *cry of confidence* to the Lord of freedom. And personhood always lives between the slavemaster and the Lord of freedom, always between the cry of rage and the cry of confidence. It lives with the awareness that the coercive pressures in my life are not meant to be and need not be. But it also lives with hope that there is one who hears and answers:

> God heard their groaning...God looked upon the Israelites, and God took notice of them...Then the LORD said, "I have observed the misery of my people who are in Egypt; I have heard their cry on account of their taskmasters. Indeed, I know their sufferings, and I have come down to deliver them." (Exodus 2:24–25; 3:7–8a)

Israelites who appropriate historical existence in this way perceive the world as meaningful dialogue in which persons are taken seriously, persons are answered, and, indeed, persons are answerable. Out of that primal exchange between groaning Israel and intruding Yahweh, some important convictions emerge: Persons are valued. The Other is attentive to us. Resources are given. Upheavals toward freedom are possible.

All those affirmations seem so obvious to people in humanistic psychology that we might miss the radicalness of them. But consider how it would be with us if there had not been exodus dimensions to our lives. People without exodus events are likely to be un-*shalom* kinds of persons, persons who believe they are abandoned to slavery, that they are alone without dialogue partners, that they are cut off from resources, that they are unvalued, that their lives are a part of a dialogue in which there is never any answer or response, and that, therefore, crying out is futile. Un-*shalom* is the paralyzing impression that we are never heard or taken seriously. And, therefore, upheavals are not possible, and life must be as it has always been.

Israel is the converse of all of that. It knows that life need not be as it has always been. And the source for life's becoming what it has not yet been is not vested totally in us. It is vested in this other One who is both attentive and powerful, who both takes us seriously and is powerful enough to make a difference. Our personhood is locked in with this other One. Liberating surprises are always possible, and they become the root source of our personhood.

Second, the exodus affirms to us as *shalom* persons that we are set in a relation that gives identity. Most of the time we are set in relations that demand, that take from us, and that ask much of us. They are relations governed by rules and heavy expectations, perhaps even characterized by coercion.

1. This relation in its most elemental form is not one of rules but of gifts, not one of demanding expectations but of assurances, not one of coercion but of joyous liberation. You know how that relation is defined:

"Thus says the LORD: Israel is my firstborn son. I said to you,
'Let my son go that he may worship me.'" (Exodus 4:22)

The announcement made by the hoping, promising One to the enslaving, demanding one, from Yahweh to Pharaoh, goes far to delineate our personhood. It announces that we are situated in an identity-giving dialogue. We are linked because of God's action to One who calls our personhood into new shape. God says to Pharaoh about us: "He is not a slave; he is a son. Take another look. He is not destined for brickmaking, but for family parties. He is destined for something that can't possibly happen in your regime, so turn him loose to his destiny, which I have announced for him."

2. The announcement that the hoping, promising One made about us to the enslaving, demanding one is that our lives are for change, growth, and transformation. We are called to be sons and daughters, expected to grow and mature, summoned to adulthood, prepared to take over the estate. The voice of God introduces a dynamic into our lives. We are invited, expected, and urged to become persons we are not. We are invited, expected, and urged to become mature so that we may assume joyous responsibility over the affairs of the Lord. That contrasts most sharply with the worldview of Pharaoh and all slavemasters. Slavemasters do not expect, want, or permit their slaves to change or grow. Their energies are devoted to keeping things (and persons) the way they are. In the brickyard, a static accepting mentality is the best kind because it does not disrupt production. So the enslaving one sees only what is, and grimly keeps it so. The promising One sees what is yet to be and waits with eager longing for the revealing of who his children will be.

3. The child expected to grow is not just any child, but especially the firstborn. The firstborn is the one with all the lavish gifts. Things have not changed much. Long ago it was thought the firstborn should get double portion (Deuteronomy 21:15–17), and it is still so. The firstborn is supremely spoiled by the entire family, for he is the one for whom they have been waiting since eternity. This exodus announcement is that we are all of us together that *one,* eagerly awaited and destined for lavish gifts. And surely it is legitimate under that image to note also that the firstborn is the one for whom incredible expectations are held and the one for whom there is most rigorous discipline. Surely that is not just a modern practice. Our promised personhood since that day of announcement has included lavish gifts, incredible expectation, and rigorous discipline. All are to be taken with utmost seriousness by the dialogue-initiating Lord. And, of course, all were alien to Pharaoh and are alien to the other forces that want us to settle for a coerced notion of personhood. The voice of the

Lord is a mighty protest against forms of personhood that are devoid of lavish gifts and eager expectation.

Third, our personhood is illuminated as the action whereby we leave the brickyard in order to trust in the wilderness. The contrast is sharply drawn between these two models for personhood. We are called to abandon life in the brickyard. It is safer and less demanding to be in the brickyard, being there with no name, no purpose for which we must answer, no relation to anybody who demands costs or expects anything. We are expected only to keep moving in mindless productivity without asking value questions or caring questions. The single purpose of the brickyard is more bricks, and our lives are caught up in an unexamined commitment to meeting quotas. But we don't rock boats and we don't stand out. The best we can do is to hope that each day will pass without our having to look anybody in the eye, without having our name called, without being singled out for anything by anyone. The brickyard invites us to such a phony notion of selfhood; it has its own attraction because not much is expected of us. Surely there is no sense of change, no urge to cry for freedom, no yearning for dialogue, little hope for upheaval. Indeed, in the brickyard, upheaval is feared by both slavemaster and slave as an unpleasant disruption. And who needs that?

We are invited to walk away from that perception of life, to give up the undisrupted life of little accountability, little identity, and no expectation. And we are invited to a new personhood in the wilderness. The wilderness is not exactly an inviting place for being a person, but it becomes the central contrast to the brickyard and, therefore, the central symbol for *shalom* personhood.

When the Israelites left Egypt, they thought they were on the way to the promised land, for that is what God said:

"I have come down to deliver them from the Egyptians, and
to bring them up out of that land to a good and broad land,
a land flowing with milk and honey." (Exodus 3:8)

So they were on the way to promise. But the promise characteristically leads through wilderness, and sometimes the stay is long. It is important that wilderness always be linked to promised land. The reality of wilderness should always be in the context of the vision. Where we must be is linked with where we are yet to go by God's leadership. We are not just there in the wilderness, for that would be like the brickyard. The dynamic of wilderness and promise is not unlike the "in the world, but not of it" of the Fourth Gospel. Israel is *in* the wilderness but *of* the promised land.

For the rest, you know about the wilderness.

1. It is a place where there is no visible supply of bread, water, or meat. *Shalom* personhood means to go readily and joyously to where visible supplies do not exist. Wilderness is the absence of all conventional support systems. And when they are absent, it is important not to be *of* the wilderness, even if *in* it. This language surely provides a clue to the work of ministry among us. We can scarcely do the kind of living or ministering to which we are called if the pressures of the present consume us. But they will not when we know ourselves *of* the promised land.

2. The wilderness is without visible support, but it is also the place where ample supplies of manna are given every day. It is a place that surely lacks the support to which we are accustomed, but being there leads to a new and unexpected awareness that within the wilderness there are supports. Bread is given. Water does break forth. Quail do fall, and there is meat. And the wilderness theme runs ahead to Jesus' teaching: Do not be anxious, your Father knows your need. The trick is to get our minds and hearts off our insecurity and anxiety long enough to trust God. But the wilderness is precisely this tense dialectic between what we want to possess and cannot, and the gifts of God.

3. Thus, wilderness is the place where *shalom* persons come face-to-face with the daily faithfulness of the Lord, who shapes things for well-being. This is not to say that the wilderness is all sweetness and light. The biblical memory is filled with complaint and grievance and dissatisfaction. The record presents Israel as hassling with Pharaoh back in Egypt because no slave was ever taken seriously. Hassling with God, which Israel did with a passion, is an act of faith. It is a covenantal way of life, for it means that the two parties to the hassling do indeed take each other seriously and know that on their own they must come to terms with each other. And the surprise of the wilderness is that just when Israel thinks itself forgotten and abandoned, just then God appears, faithful in life-giving ways. So the great gift of wilderness is not just that there are no visible supports or that there are surprising gifts. It is in the wilderness that an unencumbered Israel meets the One who gives a name and an identity. All the "stuff" is cut

through, and there is meeting. *Shalom* persons know that it is meeting and not stuff, "Thou" and not "It," that gives energy and power to our personhood.

The exodus is a model for personhood. It provides us with the counterthemes of brickyard and wilderness. The *shalom* person is one who has lived into that model. The *shalom* person is one who is

- always leaving the brickyard of safety, enslavement, and coerced neutrality
- always entering the wilderness of no support, surprising gifts, and honest, life-giving hassling

This is not an action once and for all. It is a way of living that must be done repeatedly, because one day's wilderness soon becomes the next day's brickyard, which must be left. And so it is the sense of presence and buoyancy that permits a life of abandoning and embracing, of abandoning the old senseless securities and embracing the surprising, risky wildernesses where we face the Lord.[1] And we are called always

- to abandon slavery and embrace childhood
- to abandon bondage and embrace freedom
- to abandon control and embrace dialogue
- to abandon bread and embrace manna
- to abandon water systems and embrace gushing rocks

And when we do that, things are different. We are born again!

Resurrection

Every time we talk about exodus, it leads us Christians to talk about resurrection. For we say that in Jesus of Nazareth God did for

---

[1]Paul Tournier has stressed the psychological dimensions of arriving and leaving in a rather programmatic fashion in *A Place for You* (New York: Harper and Row, 1968). He sees wholeness as consisting in (a) securing safe space, and (b) being willing to leave it to go elsewhere. In like manner, his book *Secrets* (Richmond: John Knox Press, 1965) has argued that to be a person, one must first have a secret and then share it; consequently one no longer has the secret. The same dialectic is clear in his discussion *Learn to Grow Old* (New York: Harper and Row, 1972). The power of the imagery is not confined to psychological considerations. It is a dominant theme in the Bible, such as Israel's call to leave Egypt to go to a new land and Jesus' call to repentance to leave the way things are and embrace the kingdom of God. Specific references include the call of Abraham (Genesis 12:1–4a), the call to the exiles (Isaiah 52:11–12), Jesus' call to discipleship (Mark 10:17–22; Luke 9:23–27) and Paul's radical view of faith (Philippians 3:8, 13). A summary statement on the theme is found in Hebrews 11.

us what was done before in the exodus. And, of course, the resurrection is not about the last paragraph of the Jesus story. It is about every paragraph. It is time to learn again that in the gospel stories, every episode with Jesus is characteristically a resurrection event—or if you prefer, an exodus event. Jesus is presented as the one, story by story, who brings the power of the resurrection to people who have lived another kind of life. Jesus comes among the brickyards and calls people to the risk and newness of the wilderness on the way to promise.

Let me comment on two episodes in the Jesus narrative. One of these is of the casting out of demons. Surely that has obvious parallels to the exodus, in which the enslaving power is overcome and Jesus wins a victory for the freedom of the subject. Mark 5:1–20 tells of Jesus' encounter with an enslaved man. The description is careful and powerful:

> And when he had stepped out of the boat, immediately a man out of the tombs with an unclean spirit met him. He lived among the tombs; and no one could restrain him any more, even with a chain…the chains he wrenched apart, and the shackles he broke in pieces; and no one had the strength to subdue him. Night and day among the tombs and on the mountains he was always howling and bruising himself with stones. (Mark 5:2–5)

Whatever else one makes of this, it is the picture of a coerced man unable to live the life he wished. He had no freedom. His body cried out for freedom. But there was no way in which he could get free of the demands of these alien forces on him. It takes little work to see in this a new form of slavery with a Pharaoh who cannot be dealt with.

Jesus spoke as Yahweh spoke to Moses, and things were new. The man is now described in his new setting, surely a wilderness on the way to promise:

> They came to Jesus and saw the demoniac sitting there, clothed and in his right mind. (Mark 5:15)

That is resurrection in which he came out of death to new life. Or, conversely, that is exodus—out of coercion to a life of freedom. The description is terse. He was clothed, no longer controlled by dehumanizing forces. But more than this, he was in his "right mind."

This is the only use of the term in the gospels. He now had come to a point in life in which he could see himself and his whole world as it really was, with the choices and resources together in his life, with power over his own existence, and with the ability to take responsibility for it. It is a new thought that the business of resurrection is to let people be in their right minds. People living in tombs and brickyards and all forms of coerced life are people out of their minds. And it may be that society requires us to be out of our minds, but the promise of the gospel and of the action of Jesus is that we can be right-minded again.[2] Jesus attacked our fragmented, insane way of living and created other alternatives. The *shalom* person is one who has come out of the tomb and down from the mountain to the right-minded life promised to all freed slaves.

The gift of the resurrection is that we become secure in our existence and free to live differently. People who count on manna daily do not need to be anxious and uptight about the supply of bread. The resurrection/exodus here takes a nobody and lets that nobody be!

The other text I mention is the well known one of Mark 10:17–22 on the "rich young ruler." His slavery, and therefore his freedom, was very different. He was not among tombs in insanity. Rather, he had "great possessions," which included not only goods but a keen sense of pride in his moral achievements. Yet clearly he is no more free than the possessed man of chapter five. And to him as well, Jesus speaks the liberating word:

> "Go, sell what you own, and give the money to the poor, and you will have treasure in heaven; then come, follow me." (Mark 10:21)

This is what God has always said—ever since Abraham was called to leave it all, and the slaves to leave their secure place. Had the ruler done what Jesus said, he would have died to much and risen to new life. He was invited like the slaves of Egypt to live an unencumbered life, a life of manna and not bread, a life of gushing water and not waterworks, a life of risk and not quota. He could have been a *shalom* person. But you know how it ended: "He went away grieving." He

---

[2] R. D. Laing, in *The Politics of Experience* (New York: Random House, 1967), and *The Politics of the Family and Other Essays* (New York: Random House, 1969, 1971) has developed a provocative perspective on the connection of society and order to the way that society perceives mental health in the context of power.

couldn't leave; he stayed with stuff and missed meeting. And he never knew about *shalom.*

These two stories are about very different people. One is a weak, despised nobody who was invited (and accepted) to become a whole, free person in his right mind. The other is a proud, respected person who was invited (but refused) to become a whole, free person in his right mind. Each had his peculiar form of bondage. Both were invited to freedom. Both had to take risks. Both were invited to give up usual supports and trust. Both were invited to abandon and embrace. Both were called to cast off an old order and live in newness of life. Interestingly, the second is probably more difficult, as indicated in the subsequent statement of Jesus in Mark 10:23: "How hard it will be for those who have wealth to enter the kingdom of God!"

But that is gospel for each person. We are invited to leave our coerced way and to begin an unencumbered life. That may be liberation, but it is also loss. Jesus is the way of the *shalom* person. He had not a shred of the coerced life in him but was perfectly unencumbered. And he lived new life, not just on Easter day, but every day. That is what made him so powerful and so terrifying. And he still intervenes.

Shalom persons are people who have had the intervention in their lives: A call to leave the brickyard and go out. A call to be healed and get in our right minds. A call to yield our stuff and follow him. The intervention changes everything. But it demands abandoning and embracing. And that is always promise and threat. It is promise to us in our helplessness, like the demoniac. It is threat to us in our abundance, like the rich young man. All of us could be freed and whole, but maybe it's tougher on established folks. That is a lesson we are learning as we study where liberation movements break out and where they stagnate. In Egypt the Habiru slaves got their freedom; Pharaoh never had an exodus!

15

TEACHING HOW IT HOLDS TOGETHER

He himself is before all things, and in him all things hold together.

—COLOSSIANS 1:17

It's a hard time to know what to say about education in the church. The crisis in education generally is not only because we lack money. Even if we had money, we would not know what to do with it. The time seems remote when, for the last half of the twentieth century, education could think only of competence. When that education-as-competence mold is minimized, there is a marvelous opportunity for church education. We know some things that matter greatly. Maybe this is a time for them—when we dare to think competence isn't the whole story.

We have great disagreements in the church about education. I am not much interested in the old arguments about the validity of the church, or if we teach enough Bible, or if we teach enough morality. We have had some important things happen to us in church education. We fought the battles to get free of those old patterns that were not informed by good educational psychology.[1] And then we went the route of social action and humanistic psychology; and maybe the critics were right, that for a time there wasn't enough Bible. But it doesn't help us much to quarrel about all that.

And besides, it's really beside the mark. The real issues are elsewhere. If you ask almost any adult about the impact of church school on his or her growth, he or she will not tell you about books or curriculum or Bible stories or anything like that. The central memory is of the teacher; learning is *meeting*. That poses problems for the characteristically American way of thinking about education for competence, even in the church. Meeting never made anybody competent. Surely we need competence, unless we mean to dismantle much of our made world. But our business is not competence. It is meeting. We are learning slowly and late that *education for competence* without *education as meeting* promises us deadly values and scary options. And anyway, one can't become competent in morality or in Bible stories. But one can have life-changing meetings that open one to new kinds of existence. And that surely is what church education must be about.

I have a friend who told this marvelous story about himself. He wanted in his adult life to learn to do carpentry. He really had great zeal, so he asked a thoughtful, friendly carpenter to teach him. He tried with various tools and worked diligently. But it wouldn't work; he had no skills or sensitivities to it. His hands simply wouldn't do the tasks that needed to be done. And finally, after much frustration for both eager learner and patient teacher, there was a moment of truth. The real carpenter said to the would-be carpenter, "I can't teach you to be a carpenter, but I can teach you how things are put together." My friend said that that then became his interest. "And now," he said triumphantly, "I never see a piece of furniture without a great deal of curiosity and delight in seeing how it is put together."

Perhaps that is not a bad beginning point for church education as we think about it in tension with education-for-competence. We are not in the business of competence. Indeed, Jesus had his most effective ministry among the incompetent, and he persistently announced that he wasn't impressed with competence, moral or otherwise. But even those who can't be carpenters might live more human lives with a

---

[1] It is curious that some of the rejected, rigid reward systems of the old Sunday school mentality now return in modern form with the celebrated name "behavior modification."

sense of how things are put together. We in church education might well focus on a sense of how things are put together, such as what gives things coherence and harmony and how to live with the incongruities. (See Colossians 1:17 for a statement on how things are put together.)

Now when we ask how things are put together, we can give a variety of answers. We can stack the cards in different ways. I want to suggest that among the dimensions of how things are put together are two that the world in pursuit of competence is likely to miss. I mean *trust/power* and *mystery,* and I shall comment on them in turn. I shall argue that it is the peculiar business of the church to address those components of reality, and that they are essential if our world is to reaffirm any authentic sense of humanness.

Trust/power (which I shall treat as a single dimension here) has to do with the discovery of human initiative, human capacity, human courage, and human limitation. It is the exploration of what we are able to do, what we are expected to do, and what we are permitted to do. That is a crucial aspect of how Jesus faced persons. He came to those who in their competence were possessed by their possessions. He came to those who had given up on life in despair. The twin threats of cynicism and despair deny to persons any sense of trust/power.

But if the world has not really thought in any serious way about the real meaning of trust/power, it is a rather new agenda in the church as well. The church often has been preoccupied with coercion, with what we must do and with what we hope to have done for us. We have this strange mixture in the church. We spend a lot of time moralizing in the church about the oughts. But at the same time, our prayers are filled with two very different items. One, we pray much about our guilt and failure. Two, we pray many imperatives about getting God to do our thing for us. But neither in our confessions nor our petitions is there any sense of affirmation about the grandeur of our persons, about the freedom of action God has entrusted to us, about the remarkable resources that do surface in the human person and in the human community. We seldom celebrate enough the fact that healingness and newness are inborn in the human person, and we can release them into the world in creative and redemptive ways. We are perhaps too frozen in the notion that we are faithful if we are obedient. We are moral if we play it safe. We are virtuous if we ask

God to do stuff for us. Slowly and not often enough do we learn that God is not one who bails us out, or one who nags and supervises what is entrusted to us. The good news is a glorious but demanding affirmation that we are trusted by God to live a new kind of life.

Supremely at the heart of the gospel is the remarkable awareness that when we are trusted, we sense power surging upon us and we are able to live effective lives, though that does not always come out as competence. So I want to affirm that one goal of church education is the affirmation and utilization of the trust/power God has ordained in our persons. We observe that such power is loosed when we have the sense that we are trusted. Jesus lived in a society where people were not trusted, and so do we. It is a fresh announcement, which Jesus made real to people, that people are trusted in the kingdom, in contrast to the world of coercion around them. There are surely many evidences of that in the gospels, but I can think of none more radical than this peculiar one in the apocalyptic section of Mark:

> "When they bring you to trial and hand you over, do not worry beforehand about what you are to say; but say whatever is given you at that time, for it is not you who speak, but the Holy Spirit." (Mark 13:11)

That is a statement of power coming through trust. Think of that. On trial for your life, your faith, your person. And you are given no script to read. You are trusted to stand free before the emperor and say what you must. And there will come upon you power to do what must be done and say what must be said. Before the emperor who is against the faith is a staggering place in which to be trusted by God for the gospel.

Elsewhere in the gospels are less dramatic moments of power through trust. To the outsider, a centurion, Jesus gave such a trusting reassurance: "Go, let it be done for you according to your faith" (Matthew 8:13). And in the same context he said, "in no one in Israel have I found such faith" (Matthew 8:10). This is characteristic of the various contexts in which Jesus gave people leave to return to life, expecting them to live differently, but simply trusting them. He placed on them no heavy admonition, but called them simply to live according to the new trust/power that was coming into their lives because of the turn he had caused and discerned among them.

Now this is not a proposal for undisciplined growth groups or mindless humanistic psychology. Clearly Jesus also calls people to accountability. He believes there are values to be accepted and rejected, visions to be trusted and pursued, tasks to be done. But the way in which this happens is crucial. Few agencies, institutions, or settings in our society think in any "good news" way about releasing the trust/ power in persons that we affirm to be in us. It is an opportunity for the church. We can, on the one hand, combat the competence obsession and, on the other, the *anomie* atmosphere of many people. Something savage is happening to human persons and to our notion of humanness, and we struggle against enormous odds. But the mandate of our gospel is that people be trusted and empowered to live as their best selves toward God's visions. And our task in church education is to allow people to discover this good news dimension of their own persons.

The other dimension of how things are put together, which is our peculiar concern, is the embrace of mystery in our lives. By *mystery* I do not mean ignorance or simply the things we do not understand. Mystery is not the opposite of knowing or discovering, but is indeed the heart of discovery. What we discover in power and vitality discloses more of mystery to us.[2] Nor do I mean by "mystery" anything spectacular and overwhelming by its quantity. Rather, I refer to the remarkable experience we have that the factors and persons in our lives whom we know best and trust most are precisely the ones who continue to surprise and heal us and call us to newness. Our penchant for control and predictability, our commitment to quantity, our pursuit of stability and security—all this gives us a sense of priority and an agenda that is concerned to reduce the elements of surprise and newness in our lives. And where newness and surprise fail, there is not likely to be graciousness, healing, or joy. Enough critics have made the point that when experiences of surprise and newness are silenced

---

[2]For an eloquent statement see Harold K. Schilling, *The New Consciousness in Science and Religion* (Philadelphia: United Church Press, 1973), especially 267–76, on mystery. See also M. Polanyi, *The Tacit Dimension* (London: Routledge and Kegan Paul, 1966). Polanyi asserts that we "know more than we can tell" (18). For a sense of mystery in the known, see also Polanyi, *Personal Knowledge* (London: Routledge and Kegan Paul, 1958).

in our lives, there is no amazement; and where there is no amazement, there cannot be a full coming to health, wholeness, and maturity.[3]

The whole counter-culture phenomenon of recent years championed by Roszak[4] and Reich[5] and analyzed so shrewdly by Peter Berger et al.[6] is a protest against a grim scientism that will try to have life on its own terms. Only late and in fragmented ways are we discovering that life on our own terms is poor and dull. Moreover, we have a broad sense of awareness that we cannot live life on our own terms, even if we wish. Something about the human spirit craves gifts, yearns to have given what we cannot manufacture. I submit that our task and opportunity in church nurture have to do with the articulation and valuing of the craving for gifts, of the yearning for givens, of the waiting for surprises, and of the fearless reception of newness as it comes. Those are all enemies of our modern, scientific mentality, but they are at the heart of the Christian gospel.

It is not accidental that younger children in school, public as well as church, spend a lot of time with plants and growing things, is it? We all know young children who plant a seed of some kind and then wait, not very patiently, for growth—and, of course, it does not come on call. I have had that experience myself. I am used to being busy and a bit driven, meeting schedules and rushing to meetings. With my wife I dabble in a garden. What a crushing, revealing experience it has been always to learn again that you can't rush growth. You can't make things be on schedule. Indeed, you cannot even plan very well because there are so many factors not given over to our control. Now I surely do not want to romanticize agrarian life. I have had my lot on a farm and do not wish to return to it. But there are messages here for us[7] who have discovered so much trust/power in our life that we get

---

[3]Abraham Heschel, *Who Is Man?* (Stanford, Calif.: Stanford University Press, 1965), has perceptively stated the issue: "Man may forfeit his sense of the ineffable. To be alive is a commonplace; the sense of radical amazement is gone; the world is familiar, and familiarity does not free exaltation or even appreciation. Deprived of the ability to praise, modern man is forced to look for entertainment; entertainment is becoming compulsory" (116–17). Thus is the full circle to affirm that a life without amazement is one of coercion.

[4]Theodore Roszak, *The Making of a Counter Culture* (Garden City, N.Y.: Doubleday, 1969).

[5]Charles Reich, *The Greening of America* (New York: Random House, 1970).

[6]Peter L. Berger, Brigitte Berger, and Hansfried Kellner, *The Homeless Mind: Modernization and Consciousness* (New York: Random House, 1973), 159–78, 201–30.

[7]John Updike, *Of the Farm* (New York: Knopf, 1965), has offered a remarkable statement on the contrast between the rooted, landed generation, which can wait, and the rootless, cynical generation returning to the rootless city, which believes such reverent waiting is nonsense. The theme of waiting and mastering is pervasive in Updike's portrayal.

one-sided about it. Life is not given over to us. There is waiting and valuing. And it may be confident waiting and receiving, because we trust the processes and we trust ourselves to processes we did not invent and which we cannot explain. What happens is the pondering that life is not dependent on us for its beginning or its continuation. Life manages very well without us and, given that other One who causes life, we find ourselves the predicate, not the subject. We are the recipient of benevolent actions, not the initiator. And for all that we value power and freedom, they are always in the context of waiting and gifts and generously given suspense. The world as now organized is against all that. We are on a crusade to have life on our own terms.[8]

One task of church education is to affirm those awarenesses that life is not on our own terms. It need not be, and that delivers us from anxiety and despair. It may not be, and that protects us from pride and arrogance. Now, I have talked as though mystery is the realm of children, and surely that is how we operate. Kids pay attention to growing things while adults call the florist. Kids are sensitive to their own marvelous growth while adults resist growing old. Kids love gifts while adults worry about paying for them. The crisis of the human spirit, the frantic fearful notion that life depends on us, is much more a malady of adults. And, therefore, the nurture of the mystery of the given is even more wanted and needed among adults who are yet invited to marvel at how it is put together, at how it can be trusted and counted on. Amazement is still possible for adults. Adults are not expected to engage in childhood mysteries, but to discern more maturely and perceptively the same wonderment about life as gift.

Jesus was impressed with that. He saw amazement as a countertheme to anxiety:

> "Do not worry about your life, what you will eat or what you will drink, or about your body, what you will wear...Look at the birds of the air: they neither sow nor reap...and yet your heavenly Father feeds them...But if God so clothes the grass of the field, which is alive today and tomorrow is thrown

---

[8]Sam Keen, *Apology for Wonder* (New York: Harper and Row, 1969), in his discussion of *homo faber,* has correctly seen the dialectic of "The Assumption of Omnipotence" and "The Realization of Impotence" (118–21). Try as we will, life depends on reception, not achievement— or, more conventionally, on grace, not works. Keen correctly places together pretended omnipotence and actual impotence.

into the oven, will he not much more clothe you—you of
little faith? Therefore do not worry." (Matthew 6:25–31)

Or he marveled in his teaching about the strange giving of gifts
that God has set in the world:

> "Ask, and it will be given you; search, and you will find;
>   knock, and the door will be opened for you."

> "…how much more will your Father in heaven
>   give good things to those who ask him!" (Matthew
>   7:7, 11)

He put it more abrasively in some other contexts:

- In his story about the workers who got paid even if they didn't
  work much (Matthew 20:1–16), he concludes with the
  statement: "Am I not allowed to do what I choose with what
  belongs to me? Or are you envious because I am generous?"
- In the incident of the woman who had no substance or
  reputation, she is presented as the one who was forgiven and
  who departed in *shalom* (Luke 7:36–50).
- In his story about two sons, the party is given for the one who
  clearly deserved nothing (Luke 15).

But most powerful, it seems to me, is his strange statement about
the banquet:

> "When you give a luncheon or a dinner, do not invite your
> friends or your brothers or your relatives or rich neighbors,
> in case they may invite you in return, and you would be
> repaid. But when you give a banquet, invite the poor, the
> crippled, the lame, the blind…you will be repaid." (Luke
> 14:12–14)

That is surely affirmation of mystery. We do not need to judge or
respond, to give or to receive by the symmetrical, calculating standards
of the world. Buoyant powers of healing are at work in the world that
do not depend on us, that we need not finance or keep functioning
and that are not at our disposal. It is a strange world, one that invites
us to more mystery even after we see how it works. No wonder the
folks were consistently amazed at what Jesus said and did. As a model
church educator, he caused people to grapple with mystery after they
thought they had reduced life to explanation.

Jesus worked on both fronts of education that I am here describing. To the outcasts, he came with the message and action of trust/power. He enabled folks to value themselves, to assert themselves, to make their claim on life and take responsibility for themselves. To the uptight successful, he came to disclose the mystery that first are last and last are first precisely because God's newness disregards our best arrangements. Because of God's gracious presence, we are not in control and we can relax with God's governance of things.

In church education we are battling for how we are put together, the understandings of humanness. There are demonic, diabolic, destructive notions of humanness among us, constantly being thrown at us. And the issues are not just churchy issues. The issues concern us all, church and nonchurch. The issues concern not only the future of our children and grandchildren but the shape of the world for a while. I do not suggest that the church school is the only place where the issue is being faced, but it is an urgent place. And church teachers are the ones to shape the issues so that they can be faced. We are not engaged in arguing about creeds and doctrines or morals. We are addressing the crisis of the human spirit and the vision of humanness that our Christian faith holds. And it holds a vision of humanness quite at variance from the going ones today.

The going notions of humanness do not hold for the trust/power of people. Rather, they would immobilize people, give them limited choices about consumer items, which do not really matter, while they are being manipulated and controlled and their human spirit is being crushed. And we protest against that in the name of God, who wills people to be powerful and free.

The going notions of humanness today do not hold for mystery among people. Rather, they would reduce our lives to predictable scenarios and controllable futures so that dimensions of vision and imagination, the capacity to be amazed and surprised, opportunities to be turned in radically new ways would all be lost. And when that is lost, something decisive will have happened to us all. In the name of God, who wills people to know mystery and live out of it, we protest.

The going notions of humanness today hold neither for trust/power nor for mystery. Rather, theirs is a gospel of immobilizing conformity and routinization. Our modern values depend on it, and we protest in the name of the exodus-causing God, who freed and empowered the children of Israel to rush to the dangerous mystery of manna in the wilderness. We protest in the name of Jesus Christ, who included in his power all the folks excluded, and who spoke of mystery to those who had settled for dull, hurting lives. We are not yet done believing that exoduses and resurrections still happen. We resist the notion that the power of exodus and resurrection can be silenced in a world bent on dehumanization. We are the ones entrusted with another vision and another perception of humanness.

We are invited to address the crisis of the human spirit. Our current way to speak of it is as *shalom*. The *shalom* work we do in church education concerns the balance and dialectic of trust/power and mystery, the polarity of human initiative and human trusting and waiting.

Not many are reflecting today on how the world is put together. But we know some things about that.

We know it is put together through *holiness*, which is the supreme mystery. The power of holiness is at work resisting our wild efforts at fragmentation and profanation. It is put together through *graciousness*, which is the supreme act of trust/power. The power of graciousness is at work resisting our best efforts at immobilization and meaninglessness. We must take heart. Our work has enormous implications because we are playing for keeps, as God's people always do. We labor in seemingly futile ways precisely because God gave us power to become sons and daughters of God (John 1:12). For less we will not settle.

16

HEALTH CARE AS HEALING AND CARING

Then Moses ordered Israel to set out from the Red Sea, and they went into the wilderness of Shur. They went three days in the wilderness and found no water. When they came to Marah, they could not drink the water of Marah because it was bitter. That is why it was called Marah. And the people complained against Moses, saying, "What shall we drink?" He cried out to the LORD; and the LORD showed him a piece of wood; he threw it into the water, and the water became sweet.

There the LORD made for them a statute and an ordinance and there he put them to the test. He said, "If you will listen carefully to the voice of the LORD your God, and do what is right in his sight, and give heed to his commandments and keep all his statutes, I will not bring upon you any of the diseases that I brought upon the Egyptians; for I am the LORD who heals you."

Then they came to Elim, where there were twelve springs of water and seventy palm trees; and they camped there by the water.

EXODUS 15:22–27

When he returned to Capernaum after some days, it was reported that he was at home. So many gathered around that there was no longer room for them, not even in front of the door; and he was speaking the word to them. Then some people came, bringing to him a paralyzed man, carried by four of them. And when they could not bring him to Jesus because of the crowd, they removed the roof above him; and after having dug through it, they let down the mat on which the paralytic lay. When Jesus saw their faith, he said to the paralytic, "Son, your sins are forgiven." Now some of the scribes were sitting there, questioning in their hearts, "Why does this fellow speak in this way? It is blasphemy! Who can forgive sins but God alone?" At once Jesus perceived in his spirit that they were discussing these questions among themselves; and he said to them, "Why do you raise such question in your hearts? Which is easier, to say to the paralytic, 'Your sins are forgiven,' or to say, 'Stand up and take your mat and walk'?"

MARK 2:1–9

Something happens to a society when its wealth is reckoned in commodities and is stashed away for some to have and some not to have. *Some can pay and some can't.*

Something happens to a society when its "know-how" becomes sophisticated and mystifying and technical, and it is possessed by some and not possessed by others. *Some know and some don't.*

Something happens to a society when a sense of solidarity among persons yields to a kind of individuality, when a sense of belonging with one another is diminished and a sense of being apart from one another takes its place. Some *belong and some don't.*

Whatever it is that happens is happening to us. And there is the new, powerful emergence of those who *can pay* and those who *know* and those who *belong.* Very often the paying ones and the knowing ones and the belonging ones are the same ones—or at least they talk only with one another and trust only one another. They are content to be left to their own resources, which are ample. And so the others—the ones who can't pay and don't know and don't belong—are left to their own resourcelessness.

So long as financial resources were limited in the community and were shared among us all, it was as though *we all had access* to the benefits of society.

So long as society operated by conventional, inherited wisdom and common sense, it seemed as though *we all knew enough* to get by—indeed, enough of the truth to be free.

So long as we knew that our being derived from community and we lived because we were in it, it seemed that *we all belonged.*

But when money, knowledge, and access are no longer shared among us all, but are now controlled by only some, the natural network of caring community collapses. For example, health care is no longer a natural function of social life, and the delivery system is no longer the natural interaction among neighbors. Now there is a *health establishment* consisting of those who *manifestly can pay,* who *obviously know,* and who *clearly belong.*

The point of all this is simply to affirm that the crisis of health care in our society is not primarily a political or economic problem. It has to do with a crisis of categories. It requires a review of the lenses through which we perceive reality. It asks if the categories of urbanized individualism and technological elitism are really the way we want to perceive reality, for surely we have fallen into that perception without ever deciding to. And we are beset by a fearful privatism in which context the crisis of health care is insoluble. Having faced that, we must ask if any other perception is possible, given our society and its values.

What the Bible can offer us is not political wisdom about the best form of health care. But it can raise for us questions about our manner of perception. Most popularly, Paul Tournier has distinguished between "personal medicine" and "technical medicine," clearly affirming the worth and validity of both.[1] By "technical medicine" he means the enormously complicated network of machinery and institutional sophistication that understands disease and cure in precise and scientific ways. By "personal medicine" he means the mystery of healing interaction that happens when persons take one another seriously, that resists institutionalization and predictability, but which seems to be essential to whole humanness. Tournier is primarily interested in the personal, psychological dimensions of the issue. But we need not be blind to the sociological implications of technical and personal medicine. As long as we are talking about personal medicine, about healing interaction among persons, everybody clearly has a right to it.

---

[1]The theme is pervasive in his writings, but see especially Paul Tournier, *The Healing of Persons* (New York: Harper and Row, 1965).

But when we characterize medicine as "technical," with its great expense and scientific precision, elitism enters and it is not so clearly the right of everyone. It is an elitism that defines not only its practitioners but also its constituency.

Now health care belongs to those who can finance it.

Now it belongs to those wise people who understand its remote language.

Now it belongs to those who have entry to the rarefied air of privilege.

The issues concern how people relate to one another, and we are left with the question of whether technical medicine can be practiced democratically or whether it is inevitably a possession of an elite and, therefore, inevitably perceived as a privilege bestowed only on "our kind." What is involved in the issue "Right or Privilege?" is not simply economics or politics, but our understanding of humanness and community. So let us return to some rather elementary affirmations rooted in biblical faith.

Perhaps it is strange to include a statement about God on the subject of health care. However, how we think of God is crucial to everything else related to the problem of health rights and privileges. "God as healer" is not a patron of those who have or who belong or who know. In the biblical tradition God is precisely the free, undomesticated power of wholeness who is not owned by those who own everything and who is not understood by those who know everything useful.

The primal event of God's coming in the Bible is, of course, the exodus. There can be little doubt that Pharaoh controlled all the apparatus of technical medicine, but none of that was shared with the slaves. That was only for those who belonged. You can't really heal slaves and keep them slaves. And so the elite around Pharaoh had no desire to heal (rehabilitate) the slaves, for such healing is not "their right"; it is "our privilege," and to perceive our privilege as their right not only shares social benefits but also threatens to disrupt the entire network of power distribution in the community.[2]

---

[2]The problem of "healing slaves" is parallel to the dilemma faced by early missionaries to America, zealous to baptize slaves and Native Americans, but not wanting to concede the freedom implicit in baptism. In effect, they decided to keep the form of baptism but deny its meaning: "…it is hereby Enacted by the authority of the same, That the Baptizing of any Negro, Indian or Mulatto Slave shall not be any Cause or reason for setting them or any of that at Liberty." Ecclesiastical Records, State of New York 3 (Albany, 1902), 1673, quoted by Daniel Calhoun, The Educating of Americans (New York: Houghton Mifflin Company, 1969), 64. Healing of slaves is a comparable charade.

But the God of the Bible is presented as the transcendent, healing intervenor who came among the slaves when Pharaoh would not, turned them free, and enabled them to dance again (Exodus 15:1, 20). They were fully rehabilitated, and being fully rehabilitated meant they were no longer slaves. The narrative concludes: "I will not bring upon you any of the diseases that I brought upon the Egyptians, for I am the LORD who heals you" (Exodus 15:26). The exodus is presented as not only the primal event of liberation but also the supreme act of healing—healing as empowerment, liberation, and restoration. The Bible has this strange notion of the interconnectedness of freedom and healing, of slavery and sickness.

These strange interconnections can help us redefine issues of health care. There are two views of health care presented in the narrative. Pharaoh controlled the medical apparatus and viewed health care as a privilege for some. Yahweh, the God of Israel who would not be resisted, viewed it as a right for all, even the devalued slaves who had nothing, knew nothing, and did not belong.

Israel worked at such a view of community. In its early period, still in the glow of the exodus, Israel valued its members. But its foundations were shattered with the monarchy, the institutional expression of urban, affluent bureaucracy.[3] Especially under Solomon, elitism reappears (see 1 Kings 5:13; 9:15 on forced labor). Technology caused disparity between "haves" and the others. There emerged a ruling class preoccupied with its own privilege and necessarily resistant to the concept of the rights of all. Monarchy, as Mumford has shown, carries with it bureaucratic, technological, manipulative control.[4] The

---

[3]On the abrupt and decisive changes wrought in Israel by monarchy, see Walter Brueggemann, *In Man We Trust* (Richmond, Va.: John Knox Press, 1972), especially chapter 4, "Tempted to Commodities."

[4]In commenting on "Kings as Prime Movers," Lewis Mumford, *The Myth of the Machine* (New York: Harcourt, Brace and World, 1966), writes, "This fusion of sacred and temporal power released an immense explosion of latent energy, as in a nuclear reaction. At the same time it created a new institutional form, for which there is no evidence in the simple neolithic village or the paleolithic cave: an enclave of power, dominated by an elite who were supported in grandiose style by tribute and taxes forcibly drawn from the whole community." In commenting on the same phenomenon in modern Europe, he writes in *The Pentagon of Power* (New York: Harcourt Brace Jovanovich, 1964), "The first was Descartes' belief in political absolutism, as a means of achieving and maintaining order. As opposed to all those processes that involve tradition, historic continuity, cumulative experience, democratic cooperation and reciprocal intercourse with others, Descartes favored the kind of external order that could be achieved by a single mind, like that of a baroque prince, detached from precedent, breaking with popular customs, all-powerful, acting alone, commanding unqualified obedience; in short, laying down the law." It is telling that Mumford's villain is Descartes, the one who introduced subject-object perceptions of reality, which surely lie at the heart of the current problem of technical and personal medicine. "Laying down the law" is surely a means of setting qualifications of merit for access to the social benefits, the same laying down of the law embodied by Pharaoh against Yahweh's slaves and by Jesus' opponents, who created outcasts by their rules and definitions.

rights of all are transformed into privileges for some. What had been a gift shared by all the community for all the community now becomes the capricious grant, given by the king to those whom he chooses, a special royal prerogative.[5]

The subsequent history of Israel is a tension between these two principles. The kings characteristically retain for themselves prerogatives for life and well-being, and they dole them out according to whatever fits their policy or self-interest. Prophets characteristically insist that the healing, intervening power of God cannot be controlled for private interest. (The entire career of Elijah is testimony to the life-giving power of the free God in contrast to the death-bringing control of the king, who cannot bring life, healing, or rain.) Prophets affirm that the transcendent healing intervention of God is loosed for human well-being and that no royal illusion dare try to shackle, limit, or control it. From the prophets' perspective, royal methods of health care delivery (read "justice") are seen as methods of *health prevention*. The champions of privilege set conditions and qualifications for healing: Are they *good* enough? Do they *know* enough? Do they *have* enough? And the prophets speak a word for those who do not qualify: the widow, the orphan, the sojourner—all the people lacking power, merit, or membership (cf. Exodus 23:6–9; Deuteronomy 10:18–19; Isaiah 1:17; Amos 2:6–8). Kings view health as a tool for governmental policy to enhance the throne and its friends. Prophets insist it must be a public trust for all folks because all are bound to one another. The king is warned not to exalt "himself above other members of the community" (Deuteronomy 17:20), because all are in it together.

The issue certainly is not different in the New Testament. The chief priests and scribes had carefully circumscribed the blessings for the qualified. Their criterion for qualification was "keeping the commandments." But it does not matter. Regardless of the specifics of the criterion, it is always the same. Those who pay the rent have access to the blessings, and they decide who else has access to them. The social context into which Jesus came had it all neatly worked out.

---

[5]In quite another context, Elliott Jaques, "Social Therapy: Technocracy or Collaboration?" in *The Planning of Change*, ed. Warren Bennis, Kenneth Benne, Robert Chin (New York: Holt, Rinehart and Winston, 1961), characterizes technocracy as doing things *to* people and collaboration as doing things *with* people. It is characteristic of royal prerogative generally and technical medicine specifically to do things *to* people. Interestingly, Jaques refers to such questions under the rubric of "Social Therapy."

There were those who qualified: Pharisees, scribes, chief priests, principal men. They were lawkeepers, and so they qualified to enter the sacred place. And inside the sacred place you know what they found: *healing resources!* That is why they went there and why they kept the others out. In a sacral society, worship, liturgy, and all that are indeed health care delivery. It is the way in which transcendent healing is brought among people.

And there were those who did not qualify:

- the demon-possessed: those split off from society, not enough together personally to qualify
- lepers: those too diseased to enter. Think of it—too sick to come where health is. How sick is that?
- the whole company of disinherited—the lame, blind, poor, and all the unqualified and disrespected

They did not qualify to enter the place where institutional healing happened. The situation has not changed, except that nobody thinks health is in the churches now, and so anybody can go there. Now healing is in hospitals and doctors' offices, and so it is there that entrance standards are high and uncompromising.

Jesus saw the issues and made strange, discomforting observations in Mark 2:9:

- Forgiveness is given only to the righteous.
- Healing is given only to the meritorious.

In a staggering way, just as Yahweh had done in Egypt, Jesus instituted a health care system that frightened and infuriated the qualified elite, that violated all standards of merit, and that put healing in touch with the sick, needy, and unqualified:

"The blind receive their sight, the lame walk, the lepers are cleansed, the deaf hear, the dead are raised, the poor have good news brought to them." (Luke 7:22)

And then Jesus adds: "Blessed is anyone who takes no offense at me." But it is offensive. The offensive notion is that to be rehabilitated is not the privilege of the qualified; it is the right of all, even the unqualified. It is offensive:

- that banquets include the riffraff (Luke 14:15–24)

- that latecomers get full wages (Matthew 20:1–16)
- that extravagant, careless women are more welcome than careful managers (Luke 7:36–50)
- that healing should happen on a holy day (Luke 14:1–5)
- that a Samaritan turns out to be the good neighbor (Luke 10:29–37)
- that the disqualified brother gets a party at home (Luke 15:11–32)

It's all offensive because our elitist perceptions, too much impressed with quality control, believe society cannot be ordered that way.

Jesus asks a different question: Can a viable community be ordered any other way, if we rightly understand *persons as belongers, community as covenant, God as intruding healing* and *health* as *a network of care?* Jesus' notion of healing, and therefore of health care, is not an oddity in his teaching. It is consistent with everything else he did and said. His entire presence was to affirm, embody, and inaugurate a new way of living, which permitted community to covenant and which permitted persons to belong in healthy ways.

The guardians of privilege, of course, responded to him predictably:

- They were filled with fury (Luke 6:11).
- They were hard-hearted (Mark 3:5).
- They sought to eliminate him (Luke 19:47).

But Easter is the seal that his offensive way of health care is the way of the future. It is for all. The only qualification is to be in the community—and all are in the community!

From our analysis of the exodus and of Jesus, we may state some guiding principles:

Personhood is a gift bestowed by a community on its members. The gift includes the right to a name, inclusion in the memories and hopes of the community, and sufficient physical well-being to enjoy name, memory, and hope. This is what Jesus gave to people, and we still dramatize it in baptism.

Community consists in a network of persons in covenant with one another, who have made solemn promises about sustaining and caring, defending and enhancing one another. Covenanting applies to the civil community as well as the church.

Personhood is enhanced when it is granted freedom to choose and power enough to choose. Conversely, *personhood is diminished* when a person is either deprived of choice or denied power to act on a choice that affects his or her well-being.

Community is enhanced when all its members are seriously committed to the well-being of all. Conversely, *community is diminished* when some members hold out on others, set themselves above others, or just plain don't care.

In light of these principles, some important definitions emerge that radically define our thinking on our subject:

Health refers to stability enough to share in the costs and joys, the blessings and burdens of the community. To be healthy means to be functioning fully in terms of the norms, values, and expectations of the community.

Healing refers to restoration and rehabilitation of persons to their full power and vitality in the life of the community. Sickness, then, does not refer primarily to physical pain as much as to the inability to be fully, honorably, and seriously engaged in the community in all its decisions and celebrations.

God as transcendent, healing intervenor is discerned as that force, person, or agent who comes unexpectedly and powerfully into situations of sickness and death and transforms them. The transformations are from diminishment to enhancement of both persons and community; they consist of dysfunctional members of the community being fully rehabilitated into the community.

We have difficult work to do in redefining all our categories so that we may perceive in new ways. The right to health care is clear if the question is properly framed:

- Do all members of the community have the right to be cared for?
- Do all members of the community have the right to be rehabilitated into the community when they lack power and freedom?
- Do all members have right of access to community resources when a community covenants concerning all its members?

Health care is not just a program, though it is that. Nor is it simply guaranteed hospitalization or access to the doctors, though these are important. Rather, it is a way of perceiving the world, an affirmation about dignity and worth and hope. It is a way of keeping things in perspective so that we are not too impressed with our own propriety, knowledge, competence, or merit. Strangely, when we get free of coveting, the power to interact in healing ways surprises us. That is the promise:

> "The one who believes in me will also do the works that I do and, in fact, will do greater works than these." (John 14:12)

This transcendent, intervening healing power has been entrusted to us. The powerful, surprising healings were not all done in majestic miracles or by Jesus himself. His disciples, when they trusted the offensive scandal, did amazing and wonderful things to restore folks to full function. (Cf. Acts 3:1–10.)

The issues are difficult, and we do not know if society can be ordered so that all the brothers and sisters receive healing and care. But clearly it won't happen until our perceptions are purged and we understand in new ways the strange gifts of community and the remarkable resources awaiting persons. Institutions could become ways of making that offensive notion visible and powerful. Perhaps it begins by seeing that the political and troublesome phrase "health care" consists of healing and caring. And everybody has been promised that in the gospel! We are called to change our perceptions and redefine our categories. The Bible calls that repentance.

The vision of a *shalom* community caring for its members is clear:

> If one member suffers, all suffer together with it; if one member is honored, all rejoice together with it. (1 Corinthians 12:26)

Our ministry is so that the world may become such a community. In the meantime, we wait with the promise that "The kingdom of the world has become the kingdom of our Lord and of his Messiah." (Revelation 11:15).

SCRIPTURE INDEX